# TIOGA TRAMPS

## DAY HIKES

## IN THE TIOGA PASS REGION

John Carroll O'Neill
and
Elizabeth Stone O'Neill

Groveland        California

## Also by Elizabeth Stone O'Neill

**MEADOW IN THE SKY**
A History of Yosemite's
Tuolumne Meadows Region

**MOUNTAIN SAGE**
The Life Story of Carl Sharsmith,
Yosemite's Famous Ranger/Naturalist


Copyright 2002
by John Carroll O'Neill and
Elizabeth Stone O'Neill
All Rights Reserved
ISBN 0-9721412-0-0
Printed and bound by Sheridan Books
Acid Free Recycled Paper

Cover Photo: Gaylor Peak Across Upper Gaylor Lake
by John Carroll O'Neill


ALBICAULIS PRESS
13521 Clements Road
Groveland, California 95321
albicaulis@mlode.com

Elizabeth with Carl Sharsmith On the Trail

Ferdinand

Carl

*Dedicated to the memory of*

*Ranger/Naturalist Carl Sharsmith,
1903 – 1994,
who, for over sixty years,
shared his love and knowledge
of the High Sierra
with countless thousands,*

*and to*

*Ranger Ferdinand Castillo,
1917 – 1993,
who welcomed the traveler to Tioga Pass
as though to a magic kingdom.*

Pygmy Daisy, *Erigeron pygmaeus*
Carl's favorite mountain flower

# CONTENTS

**ACKNOWLEDGEMENTS** .................. 9

**INTRODUCTION** ....................... 12

**1. THE COUNTRY AROUND TIOGA PASS** . 17

**2. GAYOR AND GRANITE LAKES BASIN** .. 20

    Gaylor Pass .................... 20
    Gaylor Peak .................... 23
    'Gaylor Ridge' .................. 24
    The Gaylor and Granite Lakes Basin .... 24
    Dana City (Great Sierra Mine) ......... 25
    Peak 12,002 .................... 26
    White Mountain via Lower Gaylor
        and Skelton Lakes ............. 29

**3. THE MOUNT DANA REGION** ........... 30

    Dana Gardens ................... 30
    The Lying Head (Ferdinand's Point) .... 33
    Mount Dana .................... 35
    Dana Plateau ................... 38
    Glacier Canyon and Dana Lakes ....... 43
    Granite Divide .................. 44
    Mount Gibbs .................... 47

## 4. THE MINE CREEK REGION ........... 48

    Great Sierra Consolidated Silver
           Company Mine .............. 48
    Bennettville ....................... 50
    Mine Creek, Chain of Lakes .......... 54
    'Cordwood Ridge' .................. 56
    'Crystal Pass' ..................... 58
    East Ridge Route to Dana City ......... 59
    Peak 12,002 from the East Side ....... 60

## 5. THE SADDLEBAG LAKE REGION: I .. 62

    Gardisky Lake .................... 64
    Tioga Peak ...................... 67
    Tioga Crest and Doré Cliff .......... 70
    Slate Creek Valley ................. 73
    'Coyote Ridge' .................... 76
    Mount Conness ................... 78

## 6. THE SADDLEBAG LAKE REGION: II 79

    Saddlebag Lake Circuit .............. 79
    Doré Cliff From Saddlebag Lake ...... 82
    Conness Lakes ................... 82
    North Peak ...................... 86
    Secret Lake ...................... 86
    Shepherds Crest .................. 90
    Twenty Lakes Basin Circuit .......... 92
    Meandering the Basin ............. 94

## 7. ADDITIONAL HIKES AND WALKS ALONG THE TIOGA ROAD ...... 96

'Sunset Knob' ..................... 96
Tioga Lake Circuit ............... 98
Nunatak Nature Trail .............. 98
Ellery Lake Dam Trail ............. 100
Warren Canyon ................... 101
Mount Warren .................... 102

## 8. THE MONO PASS REGION ........... 106

Mono Pass and Bloody Canyon ...... 108
Spillway Lake .................... 111
Helen Lake ....................... 113
Bingaman Lake ................... 114
Mount Lewis ..................... 116
Helen Lake, via Kuna and Bingaman Lakes .................... 117

## 9. MAMMOTH PEAK ................... 122.

**AFTER-THOUGHT** .................... 128

**REFERENCES** ......................... 129

**LIST OF ILLUSTRATIONS** .............. 132

**PLANT LIST** ......................... 134

**BIRD LIST** .......................... 138

**ILLUSTRATION CREDITS** .............. 140

**ABOUT THE AUTHORS** ................ 141

# ACKNOWLEDGEMENTS

As we look back over the many summers we have enjoyed this Tioga Pass corner of the universe, we recall raging storms over Tioga Lake, and balmy afternoons; trudging up Mount Dana through howling winds, or sitting on the summit in shirt sleeves, feeling we were on top of the world; long rambles over flowery uplands, and cool nights almost overloaded with stars.

How did we come to take such delight in these mountains? What turned us on?

First, there were books. Foremost among the writers who led us was John Muir with his *My First Summer in the Sierra* and *The Mountains of California.* He struck the spark. Adding fuel to the flame were Clarence King's *Mountaineering in the Sierra Nevada*, William Brewer's *Up and Down California in 1860 – 1864*, Francis Farquhar's *History of the Sierra Nevada.* On day hikes or extended backpacks, Starrr's *Guide to the John Muir Trail* and Voge's *The Climber's Guide to the High Sierra* were our fellow travelers,* and we were inspired by many an article in the old *Sierra Club Bulletins* that gave us clues as to where to go and what to see. The various field guides listed in the bibliography

*Both *Starr's Guide* and *The Climber's Guide* have been edited and updated over the years by a number of different people.

were invaluable in enlarging our understanding of the natural world.

And could anyone resist the power of Ansel Adams' photographs that beckoned the viewer to come and behold these wonders?

As John Muir was foremost of our writer guides, so Carl Sharsmith was our foremost living one. Carroll went twice on his group climbs of Mount Lyell, and Elizabeth took several of his week-long seminars on alpine botany. Rambling with him on innumerable day hikes in and out of Tuolumne Meadows in the Fifties through the Eighties, we learned to know and love the high country.\*

We often camped at the Sierra Club Campground at Soda Springs in Tuolumne Meadows, in the days when Fred and Anne Eissler were the campground managers. Their enthusiasm for the high country was highly contagious.\*\*

Hikes with other Tuolumne Meadows ranger/naturalists of that era – Allen Waldo, Will Neely, Allan Shields – made us more trail-wise. David Gaines and Michael Ross introduced us to many birds; John Sticht, professor of geology at College of the Pacific, took us about, tapping with his geologist's hammer. Catherine Rose has carried on Carl's exploration of the High Sierra flora, and shared it with us and others. Ann Matteson often wanders with us over the high passes. And then there was Ranger Ferdinand Castillo, the first to greet us at Tioga Pass in early summer, and in autumn the last to say goodbye.

\*In those years, Carl led over fifty different day hikes from Tuolumne Meadows.

\*\*Some time ago this property was transferred to the park, and the campground subsequently closed.

Burro trips and years of backpacking along the Muir Trail and its laterals opened up a yet wider Sierra to explore.

Sharing our mountain life with our daughters, Adele and Claire, then with our grandchildren, has helped us keep a youthful vision of this alpine wonderland. And for each of us, there's the other: trail companion, collaborator, and friend.

But how did we come to write this little book? Several seasons ago when we were camped at Tioga Lake, the campground managers, John and Liane Tankersley, pointed out that many visitors, especially those from foreign parts, were continually seeking information about the area. Because of our familiarity with the region, could we help? We wrote a list of hikes varying from short and easy to all-day affairs, for them to post. The response was enthusiastic. This led us to expand our original list with some comments about the plants and birds and rocks to be seen, and to include a few anecdotes about our own high country adventures. One thing led to another, and the book was born.

Some of the friends and mentors we mention above are no longer with us, but we here acknowledge the gifts they gave, and go on giving. It is our wish, in this and other writings, to accept their torch, and to pass it on.

Anise Swallowtail

# INTRODUCTION

Close by Tioga Pass – at 9,945 feet, the highest automobile pass in California – lies some of the loveliest high mountain scenery of the entire Sierra Nevada. Wonderful upland to hike and linger in, open to the sky with panoramic views in every direction! You start out high and avoid hot, laborious climbing from far below. And these trails are free of the bane of heavily-used stock routes: manure. What more could an enthusiastic hiker desire?

This hiker's guide tries to suggest some of the varied possibilities, from easy, brief strolls to half-day excursions and on to all-day rambles. Many trips are on well-defined trails, others are cross-country where the hiker picks his way aided by maps and obvious landmarks.

The climbs mentioned are at times fairly strenuous (e.g., Mammoth Peak, Mount Dana, North Peak), but on routes not technically demanding. Scrambling up rocky terrain and snow slopes is often required, but only sturdy shoes are necessary. At times an ice axe is helpful. In climbing lingo, Class 1 and 2 stuff, no scary exposure -- something for the hiker, much too tame for the dedicated rock climber.

By staying in one of the five high-altitude campgrounds, the hiker can be off to a quick start. All have restrooms and all are fee campgrounds. They are:

| Campground | Distance East From Tioga Pass | # of Sites (approx.) | Piped Water | Remarks |
|---|---|---|---|---|
| Tioga Lake | 1.3 miles | 13 sites | yes | no trailers |
| Junction Meadow | 2.2 | 13 | no | |
| Ellery Lake | 2.4 | 12 | yes | |
| Saddlebag Lake | 5 | 20 | yes | |
| Sawmill Walk-in | 3.9 | 12 | no | no cars |

Lower down in Lee Vining Canyon, 8.8 miles away, is the first of a series of turnoffs to the right which lead to several campgrounds comprising about two hundred additional sites. And Tuolumne Meadows Campground, about 7.2 miles to the west of the pass, has over three hundred sites.

For the non-camper, the most convenient base is Tioga Pass Resort, 2 miles east of Tioga Pass and right in the center of our region. It has eleven cabins, most of which are housekeeping, a welcoming restaurant, an espresso bar, and a gift and supply shop.

To the west, about 7.5 miles from Tioga Pass, is Tuolumne Meadows Lodge, composed of sleeping tents, a dining hall, and a gift shop. For both of these popular accommodations, it is best to make reservations well in advance. Thirteen miles east of Tioga Pass, in Lee Vining, are a number of motels, as well as a trailer park.

For route planning, topographic maps, popularly called topos, are very helpful. These are put out by the U.S. Geological Survey, and there are now two versions: the older ones with 80 foot contour intervals (15 minute series), and the more recent ones with 40 foot contour intervals (7.5 minute series). The latter are much more finely detailed.

Specifically, the useful topos for our area are: (1) the newer 40 foot (7.5 min.) contour interval quadrangles: Tioga Pass, Mount Dana, Koip Peak, and Vogelsang Peak; and (2) the older 80 foot (15 min.) ones: Tuolumne Meadows and Mono Craters. These are available locally at the Visitors Center in Tuolumne Meadows and in Lee Vining at the Mono Basin Visitors Center and the Mono Lake Committee Information Center.

We have provided a number of sketch maps indicating various hikes, especially cross-country routes which of course do not appear on the topos. On these sketch maps, for trails that are on the topos we have used the symbol __ __ __ __ __ . Trails that clearly exist but are not on the topos we mark __ • __ • __ • . Trails that are poorly defined and/or intermittent, we designate by • • • • • • . And for strictly cross-country routes, no trail whatsoever, we use x x x x x.

The place names are the ones on the recent 40 foot interval topographic maps. However, we also use names in local usage which do not appear on the topos. In addition, we use a few names we have coined ourselves, set off by single quotation marks.

About distances: Those who hike in the Alps notice that their trails are typically calibrated, not in distance, but in hours of walking time. After all, the last mile on Dana is a very different proposition, time-wise, from a mile around Tioga Lake. As it happens, this sensible system is not used in the Sierra. Many of our local trails and routes have no indications of distance, let alone time, so we have adopted the European custom. Our time is for a moderate pace and measures only actual walking time. Add time for looking at birds and flowers, taking photographs, or just sitting on a log taking a breather. When, early in the season, trails are snowed in, more time is required.

Then too, there's the matter of acclimatization. You are hiking at or above ten thousand feet, and if you just came up from sea level, you may feel as if you have lead in your shoes. Your estimate of time will have to take this into consideration. In any case, our emphasis is not on time, but on enjoyment of the country. With this in mind, we usually suggest half-day, full-day, very long day – or just a stroll of two hours or less. So alluring is the scenery, and so salubrious the mountain air, that we urge you to take as much time as you can possibly spare for each and every hike.

Although one can travel the high country all day and feel safer than on a crowded highway, still a few obvious cautions are in order. Some extensive off-trail hikes require a sound sense of location and familiarity with topo maps. Fortunately, in this mostly wide-open country, route-finding is easy compared to travel in heavily forested terrain.

Traveling with one or more companions is safer than alone, in case of a sprained ankle or other mishap. If you do go alone, especially cross-country, always leave word with someone of your destination, route, and expected time of return.

The mountain day may dawn gloriously clear and rapidly warm to shirt-sleeve weather, yet by afternoon a storm may come up bringing a wild mix of cold powerful wind, rain and hail, and thunderbolts striking all too close. Those beguiled by the warm sunshine who have climbed a high, exposed mountain in only shorts and a tee shirt may then be quite miserable, even in real danger of hypothermia. A weather report is useful but caution is always indicated, for it's often impossible to pinpoint where and when mountain storms will occur. For the high peaks, then, it's best to have a day pack which includes a waterproof layer as well as an insulating one. Also, protection against the brilliant sunshine: sunglasses, sunscreen, and a wide-brimmed hat.

The only insects to protect oneself against are the pesky mosquitoes, whose concentrations vary by time and place, and are in short supply on the summits. Fortunately, their season is short. Ticks do not climb so high, and rattlers also prefer lower elevations. So far as we know, enterprising bears have not as yet taken after day hikers to suggest a handout. They reserve their incursions for over-nighters, who are more amply victualed.

Last, the drinking water. *Giardia lamblia*, a parasitic protozoan with unpleasant intestinal consequences, can be found in any of our streams, even the high ones. Carry pure drinking water with you, and don't be tempted by those limpid streams unless you filter the water. We do admit that in the back country, to extend our day's water supply and thus carry less weight, we often add clean snow to our wide-mouthed water bottle to replenish what we have drunk. Perhaps this is dubious, but as yet we have had no problem.

Thus, by taking some care, you can minimize the few hazards that do exist. And both trail hikers and cross-country enthusiasts will discover almost endless possibilities for rambles in our radiant mountains.

Clark's Nutcracker

# 1. THE COUNTRY AROUND TIOGA PASS

Two miles high in the Sierra, this region typically has a short season for automobile traffic, roughly from early June through mid-November. In winters of heavy snow the pass may be closed until July, and an unseasonable snowstorm can close it early.

When the pass first opens, snow covers the high trails, meadows are boggy, streams crossings are roaring with snow melt. But for a hiker familiar with the terrain and willing to plod, the mountains are luminous, still garbed in winter white.

By July, many flowers are at the peak of their bloom and hiking is easier going. August is wonderful: all trails open, many flowers still blooming, mosquitoes rare. But that is the most crowded time in campgrounds and lodgings.

Once September arrives, the crowd thins out and there is a peaceful period of fruiting plants, marmots and ground squirrels stuffing themselves before their winter sleep, stream crossings at their lowest, and trails beckoning those hikers fortunate enough to savor the last days of Indian summer before the snows return.

Even in the all-too-brief summers, on many a night the temperature drops below freezing and a film of ice coats the water bucket in the morning. Plants and animals have to be tough to prosper in this alpine world. Nature is beautiful but spare.

Lower down, there are numerous species of trees; up here, just a few. Weather-beaten whitebark and lodgepole pines somehow endure winter's blast, but show its effect in their gnarled profiles. In more sheltered spots, graceful mountain hemlock flourishes. Dropping down some hundreds of feet below these timberline pioneers, one occasionally finds a western juniper or a stand of aspen. That's about it.

In contrast to the few varieties of trees around timberline, there are, surprisingly, over three hundred flowering plants, including a number of shrubs. At Crane Flat, about six thousand feet, cone flowers four feet tall luxuriate, whereas on the alpine fellfields many a blossom hunkers down as a cushion plant two or three inches high, trying to avoid the wind and staying close to the sun-warmed soil. And what a joy to happen upon clusters of alpine gold three inches across, and clumps of the sky-blue sky pilot close to the very summit of Mount Dana!

As for animals, bears who grow fat in the woods would starve at timberline unless they had unwary backpackers to rip off at night.[*] But the hoary marmot and pika survive the entire year. Ground squirrels and chipmunks scamper about. After dark, voles and field mice scurry out of their holes and harvest crops of wild seeds for the coming winter. With luck, you might see some of the recently re-introduced mountain bighorn sheep., Deer and coyotes are not uncommon.

Avid birders can hardly expect to come away with a copious day list, as relatively few species are summer residents at such high elevations. Many others are seen only briefly and occasionally as they migrate between the tropics and the far north. We cannot help admiring the hardiness of seemingly delicate creatures like the rock wren and the mountain bluebird, who share our alpine wanderings.

More steady than bird song is the piping of the hyla treefrogs (spring peepers) who, after a winter in the frozen mud, seem to shout with joy at liberation into the air. (It's sad to reflect

---

[*]Nowadays backpackers are urged to store their food in bear-resistant canisters, thus re-educating the bears to confine their appetites to natural foods.

that in recent years there has been a population crash of amphibians world-wide, including our High Sierra.) Rarely, a cluster of garter snakes appears, apparently huddled together to keep warm.

Even high on a peak it is an amazement, as you eat lunch, to see a delicate mourning cloak butterfly flit by, or at your feet regiments of ants in a frenzy of activity, more than willing to rush off with a bread crumb twice their size. Or black spiders immobilized on a snowbank, greatly appreciated as a delicacy by rosy finches.

Our Tioga Pass area is on the crest of the Sierra Nevada Range that runs several hundred miles from Northwest to Southeast down the state. The western slope rises gradually over many miles from the Central Valley. It has fairly heavy seasonal precipitation and is forested much of the way. The eastern slope, by contrast, plunges abruptly from the crest to the dry basin below, holding its salty inland sea, Mono Lake. Southwestern slopes lose their winter snow quickly under the warm California sun, whereas northeastern slopes hold it much longer.

Not only is there the contrast of forest to the west and desert to the east, there is also a startling and curiously beautiful color contrast. In the Tioga Pass area older red and brown peaks of metamorphic rock meet newer pale gray granitic mountains.

Glaciers gouged and quarried these mountains in the past, and left behind gleaming glacial pavements, chatter-marks, and erratics. Smaller remnants of glaciers still cling to the large cirques sculpted by their ancestors, especially on the steep northeast walls.

To cap it all, the glaciers, in retreating, left dozens of enchanting lakes scattered like jewels across the landscape.

Mountain Garter Snake

# 2. GAYLOR AND GRANITE LAKES BASIN

Tioga Pass Quad, 40', 7.5"
Tuolumne Meadows Quad, 80', 15"
Sketch Map #1

Just over the hill from Tioga Pass is one of the loveliest lake basins we know anywhere. Trailhead parking is available on both sides of the highway both inside and outside the Yosemite Park entrance. Although a fine view can be had from Gaylor Pass, much more awaits the hiker who takes the time to explore further.

## GAYLOR PASS

The trail starts from the parking area on the left when approaching from Tuolumne Meadows. It is just inside the national park entrance. A sign indicates 1.0 mile to Gaylor Lake.

If just up from the lowlands and this is the first hike in the high mountains, the forty-five minutes or so to the pass may seem a bit of a pull. The trail includes a series of Cyclopian stone steps which some years ago the trail crew muscled into place.

At first, the lodgepole pine forest is interspersed with small lush meadows which, early in the season, are aglow with buttercups. Later these will be replaced by lavender wandering daisies. After fifteen minutes is an open meadow created by recurrent avalanches, with a vista of Mounts Dana and Gibbs and Kuna Crest. In the meadow itself flourish thick clumps of corn lily and bright splashes of yellow senecio, purple onion, and white perideridia. A special attraction, if the timing is right, are delicate white Coulter's daisies.

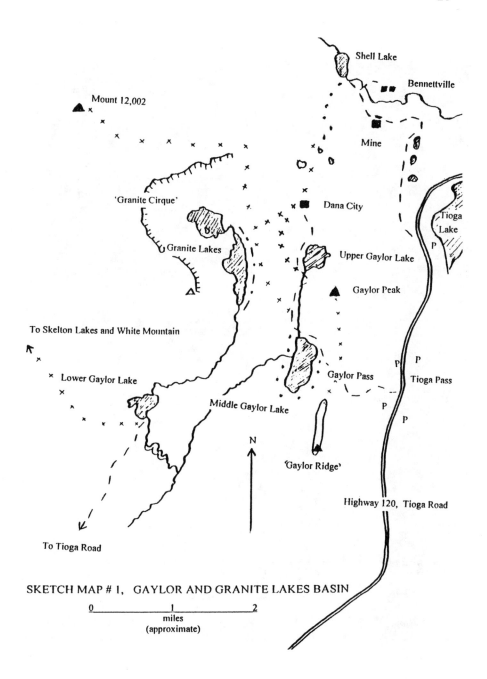

SKETCH MAP #1, GAYLOR AND GRANITE LAKES BASIN

On the Summit of Gaylor Peak

The pass is on an open area thick with silvermat, phlox, and other low alpine plants. Ahead a much wider prospect opens up, a spacious, undulating vista with no less than five sizeable lakes and a rim of mountains, some of pale granite and some of dark metamorphic rock.

Immediately to the right rises the reddish mass of Gaylor Peak. To the left, the gray back of 'Gaylor Ridge' is often hung with an arc of snow-cornice, source of the avalanches which periodically sweep away the trees from the slope below. Here and there are clumps of sturdy whitebark pine.

## GAYLOR PEAK (11,004')

From Gaylor Pass, turn to the right (Sketch Map #1) and proceed cross-country for the fairly easy climb up Gaylor Peak, about forty-five minutes from the pass. On the broken rock of the upper section there is an intermittent vestigial trail which is helpful if located. Near the base, the ground may be starred with inch-high white lewisia. Along the way, blue timberline pentstemon adorns the rocks. Near the top is a sheltering line of whitebark pine.

At Gaylor Pass, the whitebarks stand as shapely tree clusters. Yet on the peak, less than five hundred feet higher, they are twisted and stunted. This form is called *Krummholz* (German for 'crooked wood'*)*, and is characteristic of many alpine trees, but especially of the whitebark pine. Many a hiker, waiting out a storm, has gratefully found shelter under a thicket of *Krummholz*.

The narrow top is just over a thousand feet above Tioga Pass. Spread out before you is Kuna Crest anchored by Mammoth Peak, with Mount Lyell a pipsqueak in the distance. And just across the way, Mount Dana soars grandly into the sky.

Seated on this scenic grandstand, you may share your lunch with a Sierra Nevada rosy finch, while a red-tailed hawk circles overhead.

One way to extend the trip is to descend the steep and rough talus to the lake basin below, for a variety of walks. However, the route up is far easier to return by.

## 'GAYLOR RIDGE' (10,803')

As a somewhat lower alternative or addition to Gaylor Peak, turn *left* from Gaylor Pass and wander cross-country along the ridge. The highest point is almost half a mile away, but it is not necessary to go that far for the expansive views. The ridge is of palest granite with patches of granite sand where a variety of alpine plants grow. Often well into the summer, the above-mentioned snow cornice hangs from the eastern flank. It's a good idea not to walk out on its edge; cornices do break off.

## THE GAYLOR AND GRANITE LAKES BASIN

From Gaylor Pass, descend to Middle Gaylor Lake (ten minutes). Gazing across the water toward the distant Cathedral Range, you see none of the intervening meadow and forest, and get the effect of an other-worldly landscape of fantastic peaks that seem to rise just beyond the lake. Along the lake rim are clumps of pink kalmia and white-flowered red elderberry..

Incidentally, the lakes are named for Andrew Gaylor, a national park ranger in the early nineteen hundreds.

A leisurely day can be spent roaming cross-country around this large basin with its three Gaylor Lakes and two Granite Lakes. Easy terrain, good for botany. It is so open that Gaylor Pass is always in sight, so the hiker is never disoriented or confused as to where he is – a confidence-builder for novices at off-trail meandering. However, see Sketch Map #1 for suggested cross-country routes.

Dana City Mine Cabin, circa 1960

## DANA CITY (GREAT SIERRA MINE)

Upon reaching Middle Gaylor Lake, cross the inlet and turn right on a clearly delineated trail to Upper Gaylor Lake, which is dominated by Gaylor Peak sweeping almost straight up into the sky. This lake often remains frozen when Middle Gaylor is clear of ice. Continue on the same trail up a moderate slope to a group of old abandoned stone cabins: Dana City, almost surely the smallest *city* in the world.

Early in the season after a heavy winter, a solid bank of deep snow covers the trail around the lake. In places this snowbank drops off directly into the water, and a slip would mean an icy bath. In that situation, it is easier at the outlet of Upper

Gaylor to work cross-country up the hill to the left and contour above the snow until near the elevation of Dana City. Then cross over to it, at times on a snow-free area, at other times on an intervening sun-cupped snowfield. This alternative route also provides a striking view of Gaylor Peak across upper Gaylor Lake.

In 1882, The Great Sierra Consolidated Silver Company established Dana City in order to sink a shaft vertically, intended to intersect the horizontal tunnel of the mine near Bennettville (see pages 50-53). It must have taken a powerful lust for mineral wealth to enable men to endure the frigid winter blasts sweeping across this utterly exposed mountain ridge. The company ran out of money before the two shafts met. Now ruins of a stone cabin reveal a crude mortarless wall of loose-fitting rock. Quite a contrast to the masterful elegant rockwork of Inca masons in the Andes!

From Dana City, continue northerly cross-country to visit the various mining remains and mountain tarns, and to clamber up the ridge just ahead for wider views.

Both at Dana City and the area to the north, watch out for unprotected open mine shafts, especially if you have small children with you.

Instead of retracing the way up, it's interesting to descend cross-country to the Granite Lakes, and from there via Middle Gaylor Lake and Gaylor Pass, back to Tioga Pass.

## **PEAK 12,002**

There is an interest in naming this mountain as a memorial to Yosemite's famous ranger/naturalist, Carl Sharsmith. Climbing it from Tioga Pass is a fairly strenuous full-day, mostly cross-country, ramble.

From the inlet to Middle Gaylor Lake, walk a couple of hundred yards along the trail to Upper Gaylor Lake. Then turn left and go cross-country in the direction of Lower Granite Lake.

Before reaching the lake, head toward the right side of the large granite cirque on the mountainside ahead.

Instead of dropping down to Lower Granite Lake, contour to where you can see its upper end. You will notice a prominent dark reddish triangular peaklet to your right above. It has a gully on each side of it. The left-hand one is where the granite meets the metamorphic rock. Head for the right-hand gully (entirely in the dark rock), which is less steep and lower, in order to reach the shoulder above.

At the top of the gully there remains over a mile to go. Turn left as per sketch map and after ascending a moderate rise, contour, keeping above the clumps of whitebark pine but below the big rocky talus. On this sandy flank where it seems nothing would grow, yellow ivesias and crimson rock-fringe bloom among bright blue lupines and pentstemons.

Continue upwards and to the right, to a large, almost flat, frequently moist, sandy area below the summit ridge. The final ascent, though not much more than a couple of hundred feet, is no longer a walk-up, but a clamber – confronting a combination of large rocks and snow which, according to the season, will vary in presenting the easiest route to the very small final top. At times an ice axe is helpful.

A wonderful view in all directions awaits, especially of neighboring White Mountain with the peak of Conness just beyond. A surprise and delight is finding large-flowered alpine gold growing among the weathered summit rocks.

Speaking of the summit, we well remember the summer we climbed it three times in three days. First day, to take in the view and for all the usual inexplicable reasons. Hearing our account, our eleven year old grandson, Talmadge, wanted to go too. So the next day we took him along. After munching our sandwiches in the highest sandy flat, we of course climbed the peak. That night, Talmadge realized he had left his tooth-straightening brace on a rock at our lunch spot, so the third day we again climbed it and retrieved the brace. We felt we had done ample justice to even so splendid a mountaintop.

White Mountain From 12,002, Conness Beyond

## WHITE MOUNTAIN (12,057') VIA LOWER GAYLOR AND SKELTON LAKES

This is for cross-country enthusiasts, good at route finding, strong of limb and lung, and willing to put in a long, arduous day. Using the topo, leave Lower Gaylor Lake and go through the forest around the base of the domes to the right until reaching Lower Skelton Lake. Then ascend to Upper Skelton Lake. From there it's a slug to the summit of White Mountain. A milder version would be to limit the trip to the Skelton Lakes, and just say hello to the peak.

On the other hand, some hikers are real trail-burners, like the ones who do Mount Whitney round-trip from Whitney Portal – twenty-one miles and over six thousand feet elevation gain – in a single day. Some even jog it. White Mountain in a day might be a good warm-up for them.

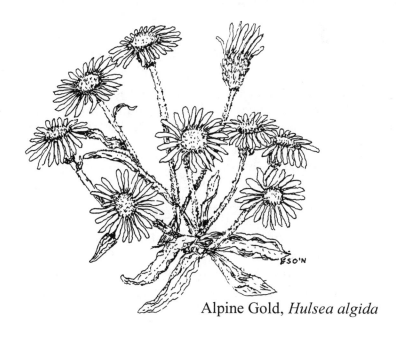

Alpine Gold, *Hulsea algida*

# 3. THE MOUNT DANA REGION

Mount Dana Quad  40', 7.5 "
Mono Craters Quad, 80', 15"
Sketch Map #2

## DANA GARDENS

On the lower slopes of Mount Dana, there is a seep of water from the melting snows above. This moisture has created several acres of natural garden, one of the finest assemblages of mountain flowers around. It is worth a short hike just to see them.

Leave Tioga Pass on the unsigned Mount Dana trail, which takes off at the pass in the direction of the mountain. As it crosses Dana Meadows, to the right gray, snowy Mammoth Peak is majestically reflected in a small tarn. Continue through open forest and past several more tarns to the left. Mirrored in one of these, Tioga Peak rises stark and reddish-brown. Juncos flit through the woods, and on the water a flotilla of mallards and their ducklings may drift by.

Occasionally in this forest one comes upon a strange carving on a tree trunk, often of a female figure, left by Basque sheepherders a century ago as they whiled away their time and indulged their fantasies. If you find one of these old carvings, cherish it as an expression of the past. The herders used to drive their sheep to these high meadows long before the national park, and later the national forest, prohibited the practice. The alpine meadows are too fragile to sustain herds of domestic sheep – Muir's 'hoofed locusts'.

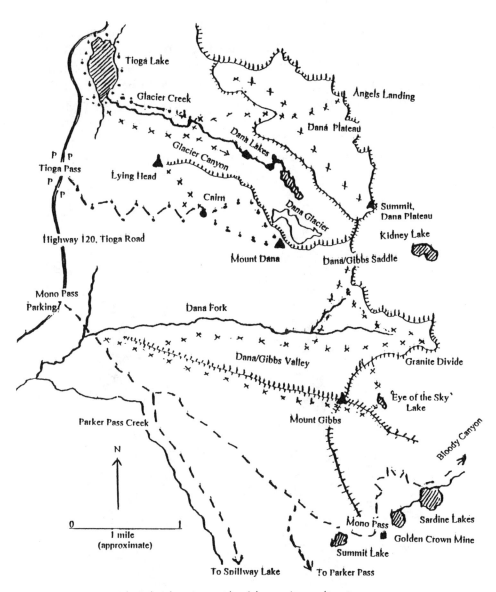

Sketch Map #2. The Mount Dana Region

In about fifteen minutes of walking there is a large green meadow, and across it in the distance rises crenellated Kuna Crest. Re-entering the forest, one sees a number of thick-trunked lodgepole pines, surprisingly large so close to timberline. At their bases grow prickly bushes of mountain gooseberry, slow picking but good for pies in September. A little farther on is an open area strewn with the whitened trunks of dead trees brought down by an avalanche in a winter of heavy snows. The gardens start here.

Larkspur
*Delphinium glaucum*

Rufous Hummingbird

From this point, linger to admire the tapestry of bloom that climbs several hundred yards uphill. Through the summer season there is a shift in the blossoming. Earlier, broad-leafed lupine dominates. Later, tall scarlet paintbrush becomes more evident, along with deep blue larkspur and purple-flowered onion. In late summer, triangle-leafed senecio makes a blaze of gold, corn lilies stand like feathery white candles above lush green foliage, and fireweed flickers in a purple blaze.

These are only a few of a long roster that includes blue mountain forget-me-not, creamy valerian, white woodland star, and yellow mimulus. An added charm may be the deep drumming of a blue grouse and the jeweled flash of rufous hummingbirds hovering above the open blossoms.

To enjoy the gardens, it is not necessary to climb to the steep upper part. However, doing so brings an ever-widening view over meadows, forests, and distant mountains.

## THE LYING HEAD (FERDINAND'S POINT) (11,409')

Go up the Mount Dana Trail until close to the broad, gently-inclined shoulder. Ahead, a large stone cairn is clearly visible. At this point turn left and head directly upwards to the prominent point several hundred feet above and about two-thirds mile away, which has been called the Lying (or Lion's) head. There is another large cairn on its summit.

Many people have wished to rename this promontory 'Ferdinand's Point' in honor of Ferdinand Castillo, the ranger who worked at Tioga Pass for many years. It is a curious formation of broken rock commanding a splendid view.

Mount Dana From the Lying Head

## MOUNT DANA  (13,057')

Across from the Entrance Station at Tioga Pass stands Mount Dana, second highest peak in Yosemite Park. (Mount Lyell, at 13,114', is the highest.) Composed of metamorphic rock of various dark hues, records state that it was first climbed in 1863 by William Brewer and Charles F. Hoffmann of the California Geological Survey. They spent four hours on the summit (a model for the rest of us) enjoying the view. They were so excited that the next day they induced Whitney, their boss, to climb it with them.  He found it quite a workout, but declared it "the grandest view I have ever seen". Perhaps you will agree.

Of course, it's highly probable that more than one Native American, perhaps centuries ago, left their Mono Trail and climbed to this same summit on a spirit quest.  We will never know.

Brewer, Hoffmann, and Whitney decided to call this mountain Dana for Charles Dwight Dana, at the time the most famous American geologist. A few days later they named Lyell for the most famous *English* geologist, Sir Charles Lyell.

To repeat their exploit, take the unsigned three mile trail that leads from Tioga Pass to the summit. Elevation gain is about 3,000 feet. Rather strenuous. To provide leisurely stops along the way and on the summit, best to allow most of a day for the trip.

The trail is well defined* up to the broad, plateau-like shoulder and its large stone cairn, but from then on it is intermittent. Some stretches are quite clear, and others are covered by rock slides.  It is obviously not maintained, although many people climb it almost every day throughout the summer, creating a number of different routes.

* except early in the season, when much of it is covered by snow.  Typically the tracks of earlier climbers indicate the way.

However, of the two principal routes from the cairn, one leads left across a moderate incline to the edge of the ridge overlooking Glacier Canyon, from which there are dramatic views down to the turquoise Dana Lakes. From there, the route becomes much steeper, and one likes to keep a comfortable distance from the edge of the precipice.

The other route at first also crosses a moderate incline and then goes much more steeply up the middle of the summit cone over tedious loose rock. At the top there's a sweeping panoramic view over blue Mono Lake in its desert setting. Elsewhere stretches the gleaming Sierra Nevada, dominated by Mount Lyell and its glacier. In mid-season, the upper reaches are perfumed by fragrant blue and lavender clusters of sky pilot. They may look delicate, but do not find the easier climate lower down agreeable.

Gray-crowned Rosy Finch

En route one notices some spots of orange paint here and there, and they have a story. Many years ago, Carl Sharsmith was ordered by the then-Chief Naturalist to go up and mark the way. With a heavy heart, he took a bucket of orange paint and complied – only to be told shortly afterwards to remove the spots. This was not easy to do, and some still remain. Not all orange spots are flowers.

On the way up, while taking a breather, admire the varied patterns and colors of the rock. This mountain is older than the granite peaks to the west, and its rocks are witness to great heat, pressure, and time.

If it's early in the season, extensive snowfields provide exciting glissades for a quicker descent. However, instead of going down to the pass, here are several cross-country alternatives, depending upon time and energy.

First, drop down the southeast slope of Dana to the Dana/Gibbs saddle. Then on down the Dana/Gibbs Valley to the Mono Pass Trail (as described under Granite Divide on page 44), and out to the Mono Pass parking area, where it is helpful to have a car shuttle.

Second, and a bit more extensive, after reaching the Dana/Gibbs saddle, climb up Granite Divide to enjoy the flowers and the view, and then go back to Mono Pass parking area, as above.

Third, if you are even more energetic and all charged up with mountain enthusiasm, climb Mount Gibbs from the saddle. Obviously, from the saddle there are many optional routes. Some are actual rock climbing propositions. One hiker's possibility which we like, via 'Eye of the Sky Lake', is described under the section on climbing Gibbs (see page 47). This also ends at the Mono Pass parking. If you do this, you will have bagged two big peaks in a single day.

We must add that some years ago, we did both mountains. Our daughter Claire was home on vacation from her school in the Swiss Alps. When we reached the top of Dana, and after some photos and lunch, she gazed wistfully over at Gibbs and said,

"Let's do that one too." With some hesitation (we were not in the shape she was), we said okay. At sunset, when we arrived at the Mono Pass parking with no pre-arranged shuttle, we elders had to drag our weary selves a mile and a half up to Tioga Pass to our vehicle. The car seats felt like bliss. Of course, a most splendid day!

## DANA PLATEAU

For those who appreciate going cross-country and reaching high places of extraordinary beauty, Dana Plateau is their kind of hike. The surface, although deeply scoured by wind and water, was never glaciated when all about it there were glaciers. Geologists call such an unglaciated island a *nunatak*. The result is a wild romantic landscape different from most other high places in the Sierra. Once the winter snows have melted off or blown away, the plateau has a profusion of hardy alpine flowers.

About .7 mile east of the Tioga Pass Entrance Station on the right side of the road is a large parking area for a scenic overlook. From near the restroom, an unsigned trail leads down to the upper end of Tioga Lake. From there, two options are available:

(1) Go easterly cross-country (no trail) towards Glacier Creek. Don't go as far as the creek, as it soon ascends a narrow mini-canyon with poor footing. Instead, keeping well to the right of the creek, go uphill through the open woods (about one hour) until reaching a broad, rather flat grassy/willowy meadow. Continue without crossing the creek (although a couple of small tributaries must be crossed) until you see a cascade about eighty feet high on the slope to the left. Follow uphill to the right of the cascade to another flat, smaller meadow. Continue upstream a hundred yards or so and cross the creek You will note to the left a wide rocky, not-so-steep gully. Go up this gully, picking a way among the rocks until reaching a vestige of trail on the left side,

and emerge on the Dana Plateau. On the way up, enjoy the creamy alpine columbines among the rocks.

(2) Alternatively, go around Tioga Lake to Glacier Creek and cross it. At first going up the left side of the creek there is no distinct trail, only obscure and intermittent remnants. Soon it becomes well-defined and often stays close to the creek with fine cascades and stream-side flowers. It too emerges on the first meadow mentioned above (about one hour). Here cross an area where a few years ago there was a huge avalanche; the uprooted trees tell the story. This time go up the *left* side of the cascade to the upper meadow, and on up the rocky gully to Dana Plateau.

Dana Plateau is a large upland about two miles long and half a mile wide. The highest point is over a mile to the southeast from the gully entrance. The northern extremity of the plateau has picturesque wind-eroded rock formations and beds of alpine gold and blue timberline pentstemons.

Northeast Face of Dana From Dana Plateau

Mount Dana Across Icy Tarn On Dana Plateau

Between the two ends are spectacular headlands jutting out into space. The central one, Angels' Landing, has also been called Sharsmith's Point, in honor of the many times Carl led his alpine botany seminars and other hikers there. All along the way in the sandy patches and moist spots around the rocks grow lupine, shooting stars, yellow ivesia, and dwarf arctic willow. Steve Botti, author of the definitive new Yosemite Flora, prizes this area as one of the outstanding assemblages of alpine flowers in all the High Sierra.

Once we backpacked up to the plateau and pitched our tent amid sheltering whitebark pines by a small shallow seasonal lake at the base of a snowbank. From our campsite we could look across to the sheer dark face of Mount Dana rising stupendously across the canyon – surely the most dramatic of all Dana views. We had picked a time of full moon, and the nights were more magical even than the days, everything white and silver and black.

The first day we walked out as far as Sharsmith's Point, where as it happened we met some intrepid piton-pounders coming up the east face. The next day we had time to climb to the highest, southeast crest and stare at Dana, even more huge and imposing than from down below, and the scary knife-edge one would have to cross to get to it from there. On the third day we luxuriated among the rocks and flowers of the Zen Garden near the northern summit, then went on to the summit itself, and still had time to hike back to the road. An unforgettable high point in our store of memories.

Note: When returning to the highway via route 1, above, after crossing the large meadow and reaching the forest, keep well to the left of the mini-canyon previously mentioned. Stick to the open woods with good footing. A trail will seem to lead on in the direction of Tioga Pass, but it soon peters out, and it's important to turn down toward Tioga Lake before getting entangled in the massive stands of willow to the west.

Rock Formation, Dana Plateau

# GLACIER CANYON AND DANA LAKES

A hundred and fifty years ago, Dana Glacier was healthy and husky for a little Sierra glacier, though not to be compared with the monsters in Alaska. Early photos confirm this. Indeed, as late as the 1950's, rangers led groups up Glacier Canyon to visit an ice cave near its snout. – much as numerous tourists are conducted into the ice caves of the Mer de Glace above Chamonix in the French Alps. The Mer de Glace is much easier of access.

Alas, today the Dana Glacier is but a shadow of its former self, and what with global warming, it may be destined for extinction in the mere span of a human lifetime. Best to see it now while its shrunken self is still with us.

There is no established trail up the canyon, but hikers, fishermen, and climbers have worn something of a route. Go toward Dana Plateau as above, as far as the first large meadow. Then, instead of turning left up the side of the cascade, continue along the floor of the canyon. The 'trail' will be intermittent and often obscure, but it is impossible to get lost. Just keep heading for the headwall. The route is a mix of boulders, moraines to clamber up, and often-soggy stretches of meadow to negotiate.

The U-shaped canyon is broad and deep, gouged out by the glacier in its glory days, and has four lakes of a lovely slightly milky turquoise from the glacial flour suspended in the water. The towering northeast face of Dana soars two thousand feet above.

Golden-mantled Ground Squirrel

There is a series of moraines at the end of the canyon which mark various stages of glacial retreat. The diminished glacier is quite minor, but sufficient to tempt the crampon and ice axe fraternity to an ascent of Mount Dana more adventurous than from Tioga Pass.

## **GRANITE DIVIDE** (12,565')

Both Dana and Gibbs are built of venerable dark-reddish metamorphic rock, but between them is a big surprise: a large pale up-thrust of much younger granite. It is well worth a visit. (The name Granite Divide may have been bestowed upon it by Carl Sharsmith. It was one of the many day hikes he offered in the course of a summer.)

Between the two mountains is a large, open, moderately sloping valley leading eastward up to the Dana/Gibbs Saddle. To reach the saddle, take the Mono Pass Trail from its trailhead on the Tioga Road (p.108). Upon reaching and crossing the Dana Fork, turn left uphill and go cross-country along the forested ridge. An inspection of the Mount Dana Quad shows that you are on the long western shoulder of Mount Gibbs. It is important to stay on this shoulder, keeping between the steep mini-canyon to the left through which the Dana fork flows, and the not-so-steep fall-off to the right. In about an hour, timberline is reached. To climb Gibbs, keep right along the obvious ridge line. But to reach the Dana/ Gibbs saddle and the Granite Divide, turn left, leave the ridge line, and walk up the valley.

Along the way, on the left, the sun-blasted south-facing slopes of Dana are forbiddingly bare. On the right, in contrast, the north-facing, ever-steepening flanks of Gibbs are usually adorned with snow-fields that last late into summer. From the snow, small streams meander downward around humps of bedrock, scoured by glaciers and shining in the sun.

From the saddle, (a *col* in the French Alps, a *la* in the Himalaya) a stupendous cleaver seems to have rent the mountains asunder, and far below lies the perfectly named Kidney Lake, with Mono Lake in the distance. At times, a powerful wind howls through the gap. (Let us hope your day is a calm one.) It will be quite obvious why the Native Americans did not make this 'pass' their highway across the Sierra, but took the longer route up Bloody Canyon and over Mono Pass, itself hardly a bargain. The saddle may be as far as you wish to go, and is a fine alpine destination.

For the Granite Divide, however, turn right and ascend about a thousand feet toward the prominent crest for an extensive view to the south and east. Along the way is one of the most extensive stands of alpine gold that we know. It is said that this is a favorite food of the mountain bighorn sheep, and this area would be, for them, a gastronomic paradise.

In returning down the Dana/Gibbs Valley, upon reaching timberline, bear left into the trees to the shoulder ridge. Again, avoid dropping down near the Dana Fork, as it enters a narrow, steep mini-canyon before it reaches the Mono Trail. This is a full day's trip with ever-changing views, mostly cross-country and above timberline.

Rock Wren

Dana From Summit of Mount Gibbs

## MOUNT GIBBS (12,773')

The first recorded ascent of Mount Gibbs was made in 1864 by William Brewer and Frederick Law Olmsted (designer of New York's Central Park), and Frederick's son, John. Frederick rode a horse. One can only feel sorry for the horse.

It was an age when mountains were frequently named for people who had nothing whatsoever to do with them. They named this one for Harvard professor Wolcott Gibbs, an eminent American chemist of the time, but hardly part of the Sierra scene.

There is no established trail, but one of the many possible routes to climb Mount Gibbs starts from the Mono Pass trailhead. (See route to Granite Divide, page 44).

From the broad rounded top, there's a dramatic close-up of Dana as well as the usual outlook of desert to the east and waves of mountains in all other directions. Chances are you will be alone on the top, not sharing it with others, as on the more frequently climbed Dana.

Rather than returning the same way, if time permits and you're in the mood for further exploring, descend almost eight hundred feet to the small lake on the eastern flank of Mount Gibbs. We like to call this little gem 'Eye-of-the-Sky'. It seems almost Tibetan, so remote -- just rock and sky and brilliant light. From there, go up about three hundred feet by the easiest gradient to Granite Divide. Then on down the Dana/Gibbs Valley as previously described and back to the Mono Pass Parking.

Afterthought: Not many miles away, on this fine summer day, Yosemite Valley is packed with people. Yet you will have spent an entire day in the same national park and, except for the beginning and end, may not have met a single person.

# 4. THE MINE CREEK REGION

Tioga Pass Quad. 40', 7.5"
Sketch Map #3

Beginning way back in the 1860s, miners and would-be miners explored every nook and cranny of the Tioga Pass Region. They are long gone, but their overgrown roads and trails, crumbling excavations, and even a few dilapidated buildings, remain. Although the treasure they sought eluded them, the true treasure lies open for us all to enjoy: these tranquil hills and valleys, these radiant peaks and shimmering lakes and streams.

## THE GREAT SIERRA CONSOLIDATED SILVER COMPANY MINE

A short, easy, yet varied hike leads to this historic failed mine. Descending eastward from Tioga Pass .7 mile, on the right, is a large parking area and overlook. About .2 mile further on the left is a small parking space marked by a rusted piece of mining machinery, with a sign to Bennettville.

Starting here, the trail is an old abandoned road leading through lodgepole pines and some fine mountain hemlocks. Soon the road branches. Take the one to the left. Along the way are two ponds, now rapidly turning into meadows. A bit further are two picturesque mountain tarns mirroring Mount Dana and Tioga Peak.

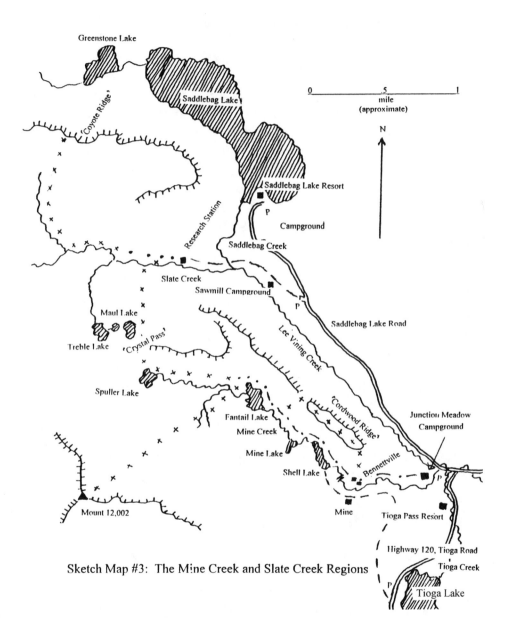

Sketch Map #3: The Mine Creek and Slate Creek Regions

Early in the season, snowmelt leaves much of the route wet and soggy. (At that time, the preferred route to Bennettville is from the Junction Meadow Campground.) Later on when it's dried out, there's better footing.

A seasonal waterfall plunges down the cliffs to the left of the mine, and around its opening bloom lush stands of bright yellow monkey flowers. A huge pile of brown and ochre tailings indicates how far the miners had penetrated into the mountainside. Their reward was nothing but bankruptcy.

Peering into the darkness, you see the tunnel piercing the solid rock for some distance, and an icy stream flowing out. Across Mine Creek stand the two buildings which are all that remain of Bennettville.

Rather than returning the same way, one can go down the trail about five minutes and cross the three-log bridge spanning Mine Creek. Continue to the right a short distance to Bennettville. From there, the trail leads back to Junction Meadow Campground. Without a car shuttle, the walk up the Tioga Road to the start is about 1.5 miles.

Note: The log bridge mentioned above can be a problem. During high water, after a cold night the spray on the logs can be icy, and even when only wet, quite slippery. (The installation of a hand railing or cable would make it much safer.) Be careful, and consider its current condition. If hazardous, several hundred yards downstream in a flat meadowy area it's possible to wade across.

## BENNETTVILLE

Surely one of the most accessible and least arduous ways into the heart of the alpine High Sierra is to walk to Bennettville and then follow the trail up the Mine Creek Valley, going through forest and across meadows, and everywhere surrounded by soaring mountain views.

Bennettville

The trailhead is located just inside the entrance to the Junction Meadow Campground, and is indicated by a large bulletin board and a hikers' sign-in register. (To reach the campground, drive 2.2 miles east from Tioga Pass to the Saddlebag Lake Road. Turn left on it, and then a couple of hundred yards on the left is the campground. A small parking area is just outside the campground, and more parking space is available near the Tioga Road.)

The trail leads up a gentle gradient through open lodgepole pine forest interspersed with dry rocky slopes and moist meadows, and from time to time meets Mine Creek.

About fifteen minutes from the start is a curious small gorge where Mine Creek makes a sudden twist and plunges downward in a foaming waterfall. It suggests in miniature the famous '*Schlucht*' in Switzerland where Sherlock Holmes and his arch-enemy, Moriarty, met their fate.

The forest opens up around Bennettville. Not a town at all, it consists of two old wooden buildings, all that remain of fourteen in this abandoned mine settlement across Mine Creek from the Great Sierra Mine. This valley of inflated dreams was meant to provide a living for 20,000 people, and is now reduced to two weather-beaten cabins.

The first, the old bunkhouse, has side walls of jeffrey pine boards weathered to a beautiful curly-patterned golden brown. The building was partially restored in 1993 by the Forest Service according to specifications from 1880.

As you sit in the open doorway of the bunkhouse, you can see whitish boulders scattered over the brown hill ahead. These are glacial erratics, debris carried here by a glacier during the last great ice age which filled the valley from end to end, and were left behind when the glacier melted away. They're called 'erratics' because their composition is different from the rock they are sitting on.

Nearer at hand, look uphill to the old assay office. Beyond and to its right is a large lodgepole pine. It has a small cross carved on the trunk, now almost overgrown with bark – possibly a

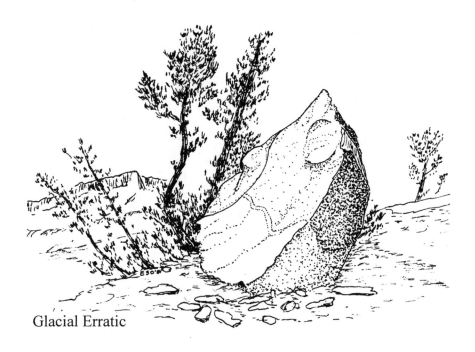
Glacial Erratic

grave marker. Just beyond is a ditch hacked out of solid rock, and nearby the beginning of a tunnel which opens into a rounded chamber. There's even a trace of an old road soon lost in the trees. Much to explore and speculate about.

To the south, Dana rises into the sky like a volcanic cone, although it is not volcanic, but made of ancient metamorphic rock eroded into its present form.

If time is limited, return to Junction Meadow by the same route. If time permits, continue up the valley. Mine Creek leads all the way to Spuller Lake, now as a rippling stream, now in fast-running polished stretches that gleam in the sunlight like old silver, occasionally in frothing exuberant cascades, and then resting in limpid lakes that reflect the snowy peaks above.

## MINE CREEK, CHAIN OF LAKES

Beyond Bennettville, the trail cuts through the woods and in about five minutes reaches a branch. The left branch goes down to the three-log bridge previously mentioned and crosses Mine Creek. Stay to the right.

This is one of our favorite walks. The easy, almost-level trail threads from one lake to another. We remember the names and sequence of the lakes, <u>S</u>hell, <u>M</u>ine, <u>F</u>antail, <u>S</u>puller, by an acronym: <u>S</u>urface <u>M</u>ining <u>F</u>ouls the <u>S</u>cenery.

As you wander along the stream, across reddish-brown rock shelves, and through small flowery meadows, the flowers reflect these varied habitats.

Among the streamside willow thickets grow labrador tea and red and white heather, the latter John Muir's favorite flower. In the moist meadows are buttercups and shooting stars, meadow asters and elephant heads. Among the rocks sprawl deep blue whorled pentstemon, yellow heads of mountain sulfur flower, golden stars of stonecrop, and the ash-colored nude buckwheat – no more undressed than the other flowers; the name simply means it has no leafy bracts under the flower heads. There are fewer blooms under the pine trees, but even there bright yellow wallflowers and senecios shine.

Along the trail the four kinds of paintbrush are easy to tell apart by their settings. Applegate's red one likes dry rocky areas. In the damp meadows are both Lemmon's purple and Pearson's scarlet. In willow thickets lurks the taller miniata. Later on, we'll meet a fifth, the tiniest of them all, *nana* or dwarf paintbrush.

Ahead looms the pale granite massif of Mount Conness like a legendary castle in Spain. The landscape is dotted with granite boulders, more glacial erratics.

Shortly beyond Mine Lake a sign announces entry into the Hall Natural Area (see page 83).

Mount Conness Across Shell Lake

The trail is mostly well-defined as far as Fantail Lake. At its outlet, uphill a few yards to the right, is a series of miners' diggings following a quartz vein until it peters out. The lake has several lobes, and past the last one some of the slabs of glaciated bedrock are coated with thin sheets of massy quartz which gleam white as snow. It looks as though the quartz had welled into a joint plane in the rock, and then the glacier had plucked away the top section, leaving the quartz behind.

After Fantail Lake, the trail comes and goes and is basically a cross-country route

If this is far enough, return to Junction Meadow the same way. Is more time available? Let's hope so! At this point, there are two choices: 'Cordwood Ridge' or 'Crystal Pass,' the latter requiring more time.

## 'CORDWOOD RIDGE'

From the upper end of Fantail Lake, going cross-country, turn right (easterly) and walk up to the low saddle. Turn right again, climb the low ridge, and walk along it in a southerly direction until dropping down to Bennettville.

Along the way are many stacks of weathered cordwood, hence our name for the ridge. They are of whitebark pine felled by the miners in the winter of 1881-82 for use at Bennettville, and abandoned when the operation folded. These weathered woodpiles, often at the base of stumps four to six feet high, are more than a hundred years old. They offer mute witness to the destructiveness of the miners and the ultimate uselessness of their hard work. If they had persisted, the area would have been denuded of all the beautiful trees which at this elevation take so many years to replenish.

The brownish bedrock of 'Cordwood Ridge' is scrounged and in places polished by that vanished glacier, which left a wealth of varied erratic boulders along its crest. Some are of coarse-

Cordwood Ridge

grained granite with huge feldspar crystals, some of finer-grained granites, others of dark metamorphics, and some a mixture of many types of rock welded together by great heat and pressure in the distant past. The open sandy places are thick with lewisia, sandwort, and pussy paws that form little wheels of puffy pink blossoms splayed out from their centers.

    The views from the open ridge are even finer than those from the valley. Here can be seen the two-fold character of the High Sierra: to the west, alpine granite peaks with much snow and ice; to the east, the dry reddish hulks of Tioga Peak and Tioga Crest.

## 'CRYSTAL PASS'

At the upper end of Fantail Lake, the rather flat Mine Creek Valley comes to an end, and it's uphill all the way to Spuller Lake and 'Crystal Pass'. It's well worth the effort. This is mostly cross-country, but here and there are remnants of a vague trail, which helps. The route is sometimes close to Mine Creek and at other times off to the right of it.

Spuller Lake is set in a wild, rocky basin and often covered with ice until mid-season. Around it grow the arctic willow and pale pink kalmia. And poking up among the rocks and in sandy spots, is the dwarf paintbrush, built in every way like the other paintbrushes, but only three inches high and of a subtle color ranging from rose to cream to gray.

The culmination of the ever-charmed stroll up Mine Creek Valley past the four lakes, is to continue uphill from Spuller Lake to 'Crystal Pass', along a route that has been used by several generations of summer fishermen heading to Lakes Treble and Maul in the next basin. In the winter and spring, adventurous cross-country skiers follow the same route.

A low pass divides these watersheds, and because of the quartz lying about, and the crystalline air, we call it 'Crystal Pass'. From here once more Mount Conness comes into view, its tremendous ramparts now closer and more impressive.

One can return the same way or, considerably longer, descend to the Slate Creek Valley as far as the Sawmill Campground parking, where a car shuttle would be appreciated. Otherwise, walk down the road 1.7 miles to the start at Junction Meadow.

Obviously, this trip can also be done in reverse. From Sawmill Campground, hike up Slate Creek Valley, go over 'Crystal Pass' and down the Mine Creek Valley to Junction Meadow.

## EAST RIDGE ROUTE TO DANA CITY

This is a scenic day's outing for hikers willing to do a fair amount of cross-country route finding, using the Tioga Pass Topo and Sketch Map #3 as aids in working out the way. It follows an old mule trail from Bennettville to Dana City, long out of use for any self-respecting animal.

Leaving from the mine, arrived at by either of the two trailheads previously mentioned, take the trail downhill to Mine Creek. Instead of crossing the creek to Bennettville, take the left-hand branch and go up a short rise until Shell Lake comes into view. Ahead to the left are large granite boulders. On one there is usually a duck indicating the start of the 'trail'.

In many places it is poorly defined, though marked by occasional ducks. It's important to stick with the 'trail' as it goes above and around the sharp cliffs ahead. For this reason, it's best not to do this route early when the upper part is covered by snow and obscured.

Dwarf Paintbrush, *Castilleja nana*

As you get higher above the Mine Creek Valley, notice on the ridge line ahead a low point or notch. The 'trail' leads to this entry into a high valley through which a stream descends. (The 'trail' peters out here in grassy areas.) Follow the stream to reach a small lake. Continue upward to a much larger lake with a heavy willow growth. Cross the outlet and go to its upper end. You will be in a grassy valley slanting gently upward, and, heading south, will soon come to the Dana City area. After poking around the old ruins – beware of open pits! — take the trail down to Upper and Middle Gaylor Lakes and over Gaylor Pass to Tioga Pass parking. An arranged car shuttle would be helpful.

## PEAK 12,002 FROM THE EAST SIDE

Several times in late spring we have glanced up at the eastern flank of Peak 12,002, dazzling white in the early morning sun. What were those tiny dark dots crawling in zigzags up the slope? Skiers! It took them hours to get from the Mine Creek Valley to the shoulder of the mountain just below the summit. Then, in mere minutes, with great dash and sweeping turns, down they came. Wow! In a world of aerial tramways which effortlessly and quickly haul skiers skyward, this was a sight to see.

Later we thought, we certainly are not up to that level of effort and skill on skis. But why not try, at our own pace, to climb 12,002 up that slope? We had climbed it many times from Tioga Pass via Gaylor Lake.

In early summer, we took the familiar trail to the upper end of Fantail Lake, crossed Mine Creek, and then went up the easiest gradient to an upper basin just below the skiers' snow slope. Here above timberline, to our surprise, we met a flock of aliens: white-tailed ptarmigans, a non-native species introduced by the California Department of Fish and Game for sportsmen to hunt. They did not sufficiently consider the damage ptarmigans could do to this fragile ecosystem, especially the timberline willows.

We found the snow slope sufficiently softened by the sun to make kicking steps fairly easy. With lug soles and ice axes as aids, up we went, now admiring those skiers more than ever. Eventually, like them, we came out on the shoulder just below the summit, which we mounted handily from past experience.

But no quick swoosh down for us, nor the straightforward hike back to a car shuttle at Tioga Pass. By afternoon the westerning sun had left our slope, which was turning icy. Our descent was slow and gingerly to avoid a quick slide to the rugged boulders below. We could have blessed our ice axes – not 'friends' in the modern techno-sense, but friends indeed in the old-fashioned sense. A great day! Another time, we would favor a car shuttle at Tioga Pass.

For hikers who consider this route, check the seasonal situation. Very early, might there be a danger of avalanche? Later, with much of the snow melted off, there would be ice, suggesting crampons—hardly just a hike. Just-right snow is the desideratum.

Mountain Chickadee

# 5. THE SADDLEBAG LAKE REGION: I

Tioga Pass Quad, 40', 7.5"
Mount Dana Quad, 40', 7.5
Sketch Maps #3 and #4
Twenty Lakes Basin Map

Saddlebag Lake is the expansive gateway to a broad basin of rolling ridges and glacier-formed lakes, surrounded by stunning peaks, known as the Twenty Lakes Basin. We know of few other Sierra areas so rugged and alpine, while at the same time so easy to get to.

2.2 miles east of Tioga Pass, to the left, are the Junction Meadow Campground and the Saddlebag Lake Road. The road goes uphill through a mixed forest of lodgepole and whitebark pines. It is largely gravel, but asphalted in steep sections. Shortly before the lake, there is a scenic pull-off, well worth a stop for the view of Mounts 12,002, White, Conness, and Dana. In June and July the mountains are robed with snow, and even later, snow-patches linger on the steep rocky walls.

After 2.6 miles (the sign says 2 miles) the road ends at Saddlebag Lake, where there are two sizeable parking areas, one for day use, the other for overnight backpackers. This road gives access to a number of half-day and full-day hikes, as well as overnight backpacks. Following winters of heavy snow, it may not open until some time in July. The Saddlebag Lake Campground is high on a hill above the lake, with a commanding view of the surrounding mountains.

Adjacent to the day-use parking area is the Saddlebag Lake Resort, a friendly place specializing in homemade pies and cakes.

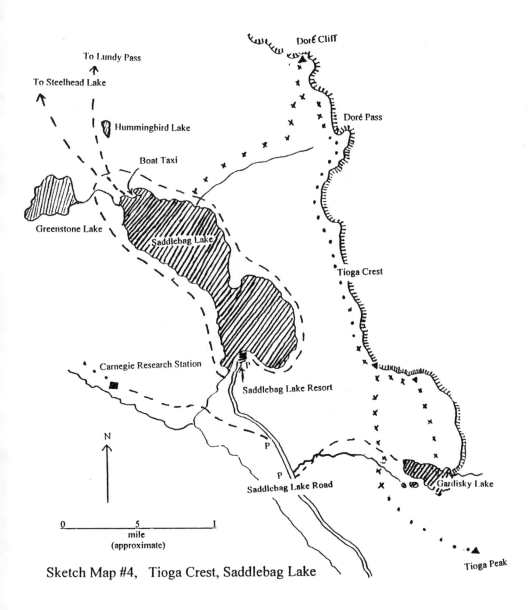

Sketch Map #4, Tioga Crest, Saddlebag Lake

Here you can purchase a ride in the boat taxi to or from the far end of the lake.

However, even before the lake, there are a number of enjoyable excursions from two trailheads along the road.

## **GARDISKY LAKE** (10,483')

Although it requires a rather steep uphill pull of over seven hundred feet, Gardisky Lake is a popular destination for fishermen. The smiles of those descending with strings of glistening trout show it was worth the effort. For hikers, too, it is the entry to a sky-land of flowery fellfields and spacious mountain vistas.

Al Gardisky was a hunter and fisherman who built a cabin in 1919 and a store in 1920 at the location of the present Tioga Pass Resort. The lake was named for him in 1932.

To reach it, go 1.2 miles up the Saddlebag Lake Road to the Gardisky Lake trailhead parking on the left side of the road. Cross the road and take the well-defined trail. At first it goes through an open lodgepole pine forest with an under-story of abundant mountain gooseberry.

The first stream crossing is above a small vertical face. Early in the season when the water is running high and fast and the rock is slippery, it may seem a bit risky. Downhill a short distance, there's a safer crossing. Later, it's no problem. Many flowers grow along the creek, columbines and white orchids, for two. Sometimes in early summer the flutelike notes of a hermit thrush blend with the water music.

At the first open area there's a fine view of Dana to the south. Several times along this stretch, as we were plodding uphill, along came a jogger leaving us in the dust. Our curiosity was piqued. Later we learned that he was Forest Ranger John Ellsworth. We'll meet him later on as we climb Tioga Peak.

On the broader, more open slope, widely separated whitebark pines shelter low-spreading bushes of common juniper, one of the circumpolar northern plants. Out in the sun among other dry-area plants is locoweed with lavender blossoms and speckled pods like little balloons, special to only a few trails in our region.

After about 45 minutes the steep pitch is surmounted and the trail continues up a green valley at a gentle gradient to a fairly flat open basin, and ends in the meadow by the two Little Gardisky Lakes (ponds, really). There is a low natural berm separating them from the main Gardisky Lake, and it's interesting to note that the little lakes drain into Lee Vining Creek to the west, while Gardisky Lake drains eastward to Warren Creek.

For those who wish to limit the trip to Gardisky Lake, a good lunch stop is on the east side of Little Gardisky. The peaks of the Conness Range spreading out to the west in all their glory, are mirrored in the lakelet at your feet. Visible eastward through the gap is the distant summit of lavender-brown Mount Warren.

Hermit Thrush

12,002 and White Mountain Across Gardisky Lake

## TIOGA PEAK (11,526')

No need to go as far as Gardisky Lake itself to climb Tioga Peak. Just after reaching the lake basin, and before the lake is even in sight, turn right and head cross-country toward the right-hand shoulder of the mountain.

Somewhat below the ridge-line there is a poorly defined trail, becoming more evident due to the dozens of climbs by Ranger Ellsworth.

For some years he has chosen Tioga Peak as his training ground. In preparation for more impressive climbs in foreign parts, day after day he jogged up Tioga Peak, timing himself from the parking area to the summit and recording his time in the register. His scores hovered around thirty-five minutes or even less. But after a while he just signed the book without writing the time. On being questioned, he admitted he had to give up keeping score, "because I was unable to crack thirty minutes." We commiserated with him, although our goal was somewhat different: to see how long we could take. We kept achieving two, two and a half, two and three-quarters hours, but couldn't seem to crack three.

Just below the ridge are large stands of whitebark *krummholz* sculptured by wind as though sheared away like an English hedge. A few spindly masts like banners against the sky defy the winter blasts. Even above the pine thickets are scattered some large granite erratics that show how amazingly high the glacier pushed in former days -- at least 1200 feet thick above Lee Vining Creek.

Tioga Peak is a great location for enjoying the flowers of timberline and above. Most of them are cushion plants only a few inches high, hugging the earth for shelter and warmth. There are three kinds of daisies up here, the smallest, the deep lavender and gold pygmy daisy, Carl Sharsmith's favorite mountain flower.*

Above the trees a rusty wall of metamorphic bedrock is spattered with chartreuse and bright orange lichen. On the upper slopes creep lemon-yellow podistera and draba. Broad clusters of phlox in tightly packed, white-flowered cushions could be mistaken for lingering patches of snow.

The often-elusive trail ascends just below the ridge line to reach the summit. Immediately over the top, taking advantage of a southern exposure, is a cluster of dwarf whitebark pines, a welcome lunch-time shelter if a stiff, cold wind is blowing. Sometimes a kestrel hangs in the air above, and one feels how magical it would be to soar over the peak like a bird. In the Alps hang gliders do just that, more frequently sighted above Chamonix than over our Sierra.

The trip takes less than a day, but allowing a full day is better. The view? Three hundred and sixty degrees of snowy ranges to the west and desert mountains to the east, with Mount Dana close up dominating the scene.

Tioga Peak can also be climbed from the Tioga Road at Ellery Lake. This involves a greater elevation gain and is strictly cross-country. During one spring vacation in April, we did this. From the road closure near the foot of the grade, we hiked and skied up the Tioga Road to the little cabin on Ellery Lake, which was maintained by Southern California Edison. Those folks call it Rhinedollar. We appreciated the overnight shelter. The next day we climbed Tioga Peak, and although we encountered considerable snow, what really surprised us was the amount of the route clear of snow, due to a warm southern exposure. The landscape shone white and sparkling in every direction, yet flowers were already

---

*The other two are *Erigeron compositus* and *Erigeron algidus* (formerly *E. petiolaris*).

Dana From the Summit of Tioga Peak

blooming on top. The following day we skied past Tioga Lake sealed under ice and snow, to Tioga Pass. Ahead we could glimpse the ice-hung crenellations of Kuna Crest. We got back to Lee Vining much faster than we came up.

## TIOGA CREST (11,521 feet) and DORE CLIFF (11,911)

As in the start for Tioga Peak, upon reaching the Gardisky Lake Basin (but before reaching the lake) go several hundred yards further, turn left and go cross-country up the slope to the crest for one of the finest views of the area. Below, Saddlebag, Greenstone, and the smaller lakes. Beyond, an alpine panorama of mountains: 12,002, White, Conness, North Peak, Shepherds Crest, and Excelsior. In sharp contrast, the dry desert mountains to the east, and a glimpse southeast to the White Mountains. This seemingly dry heap of rock is also a garden of alpine flowers.

Northwards there are remnants of an old prospectors' trail. It's to the left just below the crest, and makes travel along the broad but rocky saddleback easier. In about two miles one reaches Doré Pass and can look down the extremely steep drop into Warren Canyon. How can this be called a pass?

Just ahead is Doré Cliff sticking up like a hatchet against the sky. It is indeed a steep precipice on the north side. However, the south side entails an easy rock scramble up a moderate slope of talus for an additional several hundred feet -- well worth it for the mountain panorama in every direction and an overlook into gold and rusty Lundy Canyon, site of a famous old abandoned mine.

To return, descend the broad grassy valley to Saddlebag Lake. (See Sketch Map #4.) It is easier going near the stream. For the final descent through the woods, stay on the north side of the stream, as the left-hand side has steep rocky sections more difficult to negotiate. Upon reaching the lakeside trail, turn left to return to the trailhead. Alternatively, upon reaching the trail walk *right* (north) to the boat landing for a ride back.

Doré Cliff

For a shorter trip, upon reaching Tioga Crest, return the same way. But keep to the left in descending. Head for the trail in the lake basin. If you veer too far to the right, you will encounter steep cliffs and miss the trail. An advantage of this routing is to return to the same trailhead as the start.

There is yet another option. Upon reaching the crest, go along it to the right (easterly), heading for another high point about a third of a mile away. From here descend a broad, flowery slope to Gardisky Lake. On this hillside, seeping snow-melt waters an acre or more of golden arnica in season.

Arnica, *Arnica sp.*

## SLATE CREEK VALLEY

This is a leisurely day's trip, with little elevation gain. It goes through a variety of habitats: forest, meadow, streamside, with a backdrop of snowy alpine peaks, provoking an urge to wander higher.

To get started, 1.7 miles up the Saddlebag Lake Road from the Tioga Road, to the left, is the parking for the Sawmill Walk-in Campground in Slate Creek Valley. This is the trailhead.

Regarding the various tributaries of Lee Vining Creek, there is a confusion of nomenclature. The official Tioga Pass Quadrangle names only one of the four tributaries composing Lee Vining Creek, namely, Mine Creek, which enters it at Junction Meadow.

On the other hand, the local usage Twenty Lakes Basin Map names the other three, and calls the branch coming out of Saddlebag Lake, Saddlebag Creek; the branch entering Saddlebag Creek from the Maul Lake Area, Slate Creek; and the branch from Tioga Lake, Tioga Creek.

We think there is something to be said for these further distinctions, helpful in specifying particular locations. So when we describe a hike up Slate Creek Valley, we refer to that area along Slate Creek on the Twenty Lake Basin local map.

The walk-in campground, with twelve widely separated sites, is beautifully situated on a shelf above the creek. Looking up-valley, the sky is dominated by Mount Conness with long spurs like immense flying buttresses. To the left are 12,002 and White Mountain. The latter has a huge glacial cirque on its east flank.

Shortly past the campground there is a sign designating the Harvey Monroe Hall Natural Area. This large area within the Hoover Wilderness has been set aside for ecological research, and although no camping is allowed, hikers are welcome. A few minutes later is the Saddlebag Creek crossing. The difficulty will vary with the magnitude of the flow.

About half an hour from the parking area is the former Experimental Station of the Department of Plant Biology of the Carnegie Institute, Washington, D.C. Some years ago, the institute conducted parallel studies at three different elevations to test the relative effects of heredity and climate on plants – here at about 10,000 feet, at Mather, California at 4,600 feet, and in Palo Alto almost at sea level.

At one time college students used to spend the summer here doing much of the work. For some, this was their first western mountain experience, and in spite of mosquitoes, they reported a wonderful adventure. Time off could be spent doing the peaks and falling in love.

Now, several decades later, many are grandparents, the buildings that housed them are sagging, the experimental garden has gone wild, and even the type of experiment is now a bit old-fashioned in this new age of biotechnology with its trans-gene manipulation marvels.

In the damp area around the station grow purple swamp onion and several different kinds of senecio, also known as butterweed, all bright sunshine yellow. From here, an intermittent trail continues up to the head of Slate Creek Valley. After some distance, a fisherman's trail follows the creek, while an old mining road veers right. Follow the 'road', which at best is but a trail, sometimes dwindling to one track overgrown by meadow, sometimes disappearing altogether, only to reappear later on.

Near the head of the valley, the scenery becomes more and more alpine, opening into a meadowy parkland with clumps of picturesque whitebarks here and there. Slate Creek further divides into smaller streams sparkling in the sun.

To the sybarite who accepts the suggestion of a leisurely day, this destination is just fine. After one picks a comfy spot to settle down, the pinot grigio is tucked into a snowbank for chilling. The *chèvre* cheese and *pain-complet* from Trader Joe's comes out of the day pack. Also some grapes from the foothills of the Andes in Chile. Plebian slices of chicken breast appear. Omar Khayyám, where are you? Ah, wilderness is paradise enow!

Research Station, Carnegie Institute, Slate Creek Valley

But for those blessed or cursed with more alpine genes, the heights all around exert an irresistible tug. Such enticing choices: a bushwhack up to Alpine Lake, a scramble to Bighorn Lake seeking a leviathan of a trout, or return via 'Crystal Pass' to the Mine Creek Valley. Or, like us, a trek up 'Coyote Ridge', a land above the trees.

## 'COYOTE RIDGE' (about 11,000')

One day we were starting up this slope with our friend, Ann, and her large black dog. Suddenly a pack of coyotes set up a series of howls, enticing the dog to charge uphill in pursuit. Knowing this could be a typical coyote ambush, we shouted mightily and finally persuaded the dog to give up the chase. Ever since, that hillside has been 'Coyote Ridge' to us.

To get started, go up Slate Creek Valley until the branch of the creek coming down the cliffs from Alpine Lake is visible and close ahead. Another branch tumbles down from 'Coyote Ridge' to the right. Somewhat to the right of this branch, pick the easiest gradient and go up. It's fairly steep for some distance, but eases off later.

Among the trees a little way up and to the right you may make the astonishing discovery of an old rusted compressor, tons of iron high on the hillside suggesting a tremendous expenditure of effort – much sweat but no riches.

Once the trees are left behind, pass some rock-rimmed tarns (or snowfields, depending on the season), mirroring snowy White Mountain to the south, and reach the ridge for a greatly expanded view down over Saddlebag and Greenstone Lakes, and across to North Peak, Shepherds Crest, and Excelsior. Across Saddlebag is Tioga Crest with the abrupt hatchet of Doré Cliff cleaving the sky.

Going down again, be sure to keep to the right, not far from the stream. A descent farther to the left soon encounters steep cliffs.

White Mountain From 'Coyote Ridge'

## MOUNT CONNESS (12,590)

Mount Conness has more of a human history than any of its fellow summits. In 1863, the Whitney Geological Survey of California named it for John Conness (1821-1909), an Irishman who had become a California Senator. He was instrumental in creating this survey. He also introduced the bill that granted Yosemite Valley and the Mariposa Grove to the state.

Later, in the summers of 1879, 1887, and 1890, the summit was used as a survey station by parties under George Davidson for the United States Coast and Geodetic Survey. Each man stayed on top three days at a time – quite enough before heading to a lower campsite to warm up and rest before climbing again.

For climbers willing to put in a long day, Mt. Conness can be climbed from the Slate Creek Valley via romantic Alpine Lake at the base of soaring cliffs. Just getting up to Alpine Lake is a bit of a scramble. For some years, this was the route Ranger Carl Sharsmith followed when he led parties up the mountain, often arriving back in Tuolumne Meadows after dark, in spite of an early start.

Kestrel

# 6. THE SADDLEBAG LAKE REGION: II

Tioga Pass Quad, 40', 7.5"
Sketch Maps #4 and #5
Twenty Lakes Basin Map

## SADDLEBAG LAKE CIRCUIT

If time is limited to half a day or less, hiking the circuit of Saddlebag Lake takes little effort and provides fine alpine scenery. The 'trail' (actually, the old mining road) starts at the day-use parking by the Saddlebag Lake Resort and goes along the east side of the lake to its upper end, where it divides into three different routes.

At the start, the trail drops down to a moist meadow which, a few years ago, provided a fine chorus of frog music. Now, alas, with a world-wide crash of frog populations, this pleasure is much diminished.

Soon after starting, look back at Mounts 12,002, White, and Conness, often beautifully mirrored in the lake. Later these will disappear behind a reddish ridge. As compensation, North Peak, Shepherd's Crest and Excelsior come into view.

These distant mountain prospects are nicely complemented by close-up floral displays. About twenty-five minutes out, a stream seeps down the mountainside watering a long broad swathe of golden arnica and monkey flower, purple monkshood, scarlet *miniata* paintbrush, orchid-pink wild onions, and the white torches of corn lily. The road is edged with green-gold moss.

At the upper end of the lake is a rustic cabin, used in recent years by the wilderness ranger. It faces down the lake toward Mount Dana rising grandly into the sky.

Shortly after the cabin, there's a three-way junction. The right branch is signed to Lundy Canyon. Straight ahead the trail (the old mining road) goes on to Steelhead Lake. The left branch leads down to the boat dock at the upper end of the lake. Take this branch.

In order to circle the lake, at this point continue along the lakeshore, find a place to cross the inlet stream, and meet the trail going south down the west side of the lake. This area has glowing displays of scarlet meadow paintbrush. The trail, in sharp contrast to the one on the east side, is narrow, rough, and rocky much of the way and provides less spectacular views. At the outlet, cross the top of the dam to get back to the parking area.

California gulls, who pass the winter enjoying big city life in San Francisco, spend summers at Mono Lake raising a family. They soar into the mountains and are often seen wheeling overhead looking for a fish or, better yet, a handout from the fishermen. They can be readily distinguished from the occasional Caspian terns, also mostly white, but larger and with brilliant scarlet bills.

California Gull

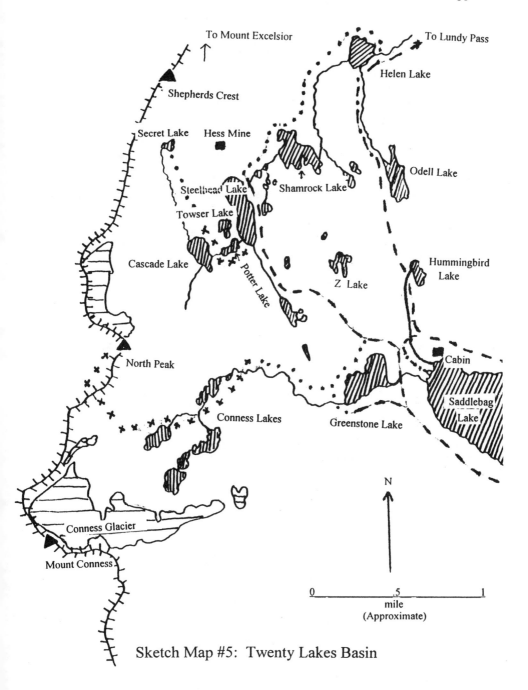

Sketch Map #5: Twenty Lakes Basin

## DORE CLIFF FROM SADDLEBAG LAKE

This trip is the reverse of the one captioned "Tioga Crest and Doré Cliff", described on page 70. However, it only goes as far as Doré Cliff rather than all the way back to the Gardisky Lake Trailhead.

About three quarters of the way along the lakeshore, the stream from Tioga Crest comes across the trail. Cross it. At this point, to climb up to Tioga Crest and on to Doré Cliff, go cross-country uphill through the woods to the left of the stream. (The right side is much steeper.) After the forest there's an open meadow upland slanting up to Tioga Crest. From there climb Doré Cliff and return the same way.

## CONNESS LAKES

When mountaineers describe their journeys, they often invoke images of magic places like the inner sanctum of Nanda Devi or an imaginary Shangri La. Frequently they tell of passing through a secret entry to reach such enchantments.

Here in our own High Sierra Twenty Lakes Basin, there is, in a way, such a special place: the Conness Lakes nestled below the imposing northeast wall of Mount Conness and its glacier.

Hyla Treefrog

Many gemlike Sierran spots take several days to reach; in other mountain ranges, days or weeks. But far from a laborious trek into the wilds of the Tibetan Himalaya, the Conness Lakes are easily accessible, almost too much so. How can such an exquisite alpine sanctuary be only several hours from a road-head?

To go, (see Sketch Map #5) start at the three-way junction mentioned on page 80. Stay on the trail (old mining road) towards Steelhead Lake, and shortly come to a stand with a sign-in sheet. The route then comes close to the shore of Greenstone Lake, and a number of side paths lead down to the lake shore. The most convenient is where the main trail is closest to the lake.

Drop down to the shore and take the trail towards the upper end of the lake. Much of the way, the trail is overgrown by meadow and is not distinct. Often it is wet and swarming with moisture-loving plants: elephant heads, meadow asters, and shooting stars.

Towards the upper end of the lake, a rocky mass rises abruptly out of the water. Keep to the right. A short distance ahead is a sign announcing entry into the Hall Natural Area. Here the trail, often indistinct, parallels the stream.

After a short uphill stretch beside rushing cascades, there is another flat meadowy area. A waterfall comes tumbling down a cliff face ahead. The 'trail' starts up the rather steep granite slabs well to the right of the waterfall. (Notice how the granite is criss-crossed by white dikes.) The trail fades out on the granite slabs. At this point, hikers choose various routes to get to the lake basin above. We prefer gaining elevation on the grassy and rocky slope to the right of the slabs.

At about level with the top of the falls and below some small cliffs, traverse left across the slabs on a moderate incline to a ledge, along which a mysterious water-course runs. It is mysterious because obviously man-made, perhaps a flume from some forgotten mining venture.

Here, depending upon snow conditions, work your way upwards into the level basin in which the two lowest of the Conness Lakes are located.

From a valley whose eastern flank is dominated by the rusty rounded contours of Tioga Crest, one has passed through pale granite portals -- the Conness version of the secret entry into a magic alpine world. Ahead, bathed in shimmering radiant light, the basin has an other-worldly austere beauty. It is enclosed like a cathedral between North Peak's fluted flanks and Mount Conness straddling the skyline on many long spurs.

Once in the basin, cross the stream on conveniently located rocks. Go left around the first lake and follow the inlet (a series of small cascades) up to the next lake. The three higher lakes are readily reached.

The lakes are a lovely milky turquoise that shows their origin in a glacier; finely ground rock flour gives their special color. The bedrock is composed of Cathedral Peak Granodiorite, pale cream or slightly rosy and studded with enormous feldspar crystals, the whole polished smooth by bygone glaciers and glittering in the sun. Walking across these shining pavements, we feel we have entered an enchanted realm.

Note: The route up Mount Conness via the Upper Conness Lake and Conness Glacier is a one-day climb, but more appropriate for the well-equipped climber than for the unassisted hiker. See *The Climber's Guide to the High Sierra.*

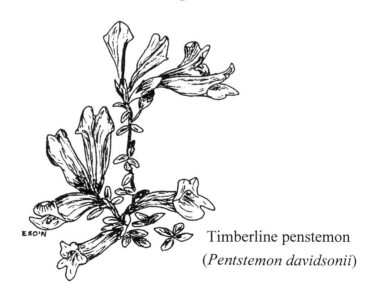

Timberline penstemon
(*Pentstemon davidsonii*)

Mount Conness From Shoulder of North Peak

## NORTH PEAK (12,242')

This is a full-day trip from Saddlebag Lake up one of the most dramatic mountains in the region, yet it can be climbed by a hiker on a Class 2 route. Valuable time can be saved by taking the boat taxi to the upper end of the lake. Returning to the boat dock in time for the last run back will save an additional hour.

Follow the route described above to the Conness Lakes. From the Lower Conness Lake follow the intake stream on the left side to Upper Conness Lake – the one just at the foot of North Peak. Cross the outlet and start up the slope. Traverse left above the clumps of whitebark until the lowest notch on the skyline is directly above. Scramble up the loose scree and sand to reach this notch. This is not easy, for it seems at times you lose one step for each two gained. A walking stick is a big help.

Upon reaching the notch, turn right up the broad sloping shoulder of North Peak. This is a moderately inclined alpine fell-field of cushion-plants, leading to the rocky narrow top.

The view? One of the best! Far below, the turquoise Conness Lakes, and thrusting up just across the way, the spectacular peak of Conness. To the north and east, you can gaze down dizzying steep cliffs and snow and ice couloirs which hardier souls with more technical skill use to ascend to the summit. And, sitting up there munching your sandwiches, you have a sense of being on top of the world.

In descending from the notch, keep left on the same gradient as in coming up. Avoid going too far to the right, as below it becomes steeper and cliffier.

## SECRET LAKE

This lake is perfectly named, for much of the time it is indeed a secret, completely invisible. After winters of heavy snow it remains covered until late in the summer. The lake is

Mount Conness From Summit of North Peak

dramatically located on a high shelf above the Twenty Lakes Basin, just below Shepherds Crest. About an hour and a half from Steelhead Lake, and well worth the moderate additional climb of almost six hundred feet.

The route: from the upper end of Saddlebag Lake, another half hour along the mine road is Steelhead Lake. Along the way, North Peak rises ever higher and more awesome. It is reflected in many small pools set in an open landscape with scattered stands of whitebark pine. The trail winds between banks of dark rock liberally decorated with whitish granitic erratics dropped by retreating glaciers. Pride of the mountain and mule ears are a symphony of magenta and gold.

A couple of hundred feet before reaching Steelhead Lake, there is a trail to the left which goes downhill to a small stream, crosses it, and ascends a slight rise, then abruptly drops down to another stream. At this point there is a trail heading south. Do not take it, as it leads in the opposite direction from the destination. Rather, turn right and head off cross-country toward Shepherds Crest, going parallel to and somewhat above Potter Lake. Some distance ahead is a small cascade flowing into Potter. It's the outlet of Cascade Lake. Head for it.

The entire basin is paved with rolling granitic bedrock. The size of the gigantic feldspar crystals embedded in it tells us that the rock cooled very slowly from a molten state deep within the earth. Ages later, after the cover of sedimentary rock had been eroded away, glaciers scoured and polished the granite, creating an elegant radiant floor worthy of a baroque palace or a great cathedral. Now pools of melting snow rest placidly in the depressions.

Upon reaching the outlet of Cascade Lake, cross the stream just above the cascade, where there is usually a rock-step crossing, and head for the upper end of the lake. There, off to the left, a stream bubbles down the steep hillside into the lake. It's the outlet from Secret Lake. Walking uphill well to the right of this stream, you will meet a well-defined trail which soon reaches the outlet stream and parallels it.

Although on a fairly steep slope, the route is meadowy and willowy, and in season ablaze with hundreds of meadow paintbrush. Mountain hemlocks, somewhat dwarfed with large snow-mats at their bases, dot the hillside. And there are five members of the circumpolar arctic-alpine heath family: white-flowered labrador tea, red and white heather, pink kalmia, and a ground-cover of snow bilberry whose leaves will turn vermilion in autumn. Indeed, this is a most beautiful alpine Sierran landscape – as though a gardener with impeccable taste and an unlimited budget had realized his heart's desire.

As you gain elevation, the north wall of North Peak, streaked with almost vertical snow and ice couloirs, grows ever-more impressive. Nice to sit down for a breather now and then and take it in.

The trail winds among rocks and willows up to an open bench where you will either see Secret Lake or the snowfield under which it lies.

North Peak Across Secret Lake

Around the lake is a jumble of huge boulders, and among them clumps of whitebark pine offer shelter from a cold wind, a welcome lunchroom. A marmot may pop out looking for whatever weird humans are invading his domain, and not averse to accepting a snack himself. Away to the north, south, and east spreads an expansive vision of peaks and valleys.

Blocking the view to the west is a rather steep cliff. A backpacker's route threads up and over it, to descend to the McCabe Lakes on the other side.

From Secret Lake, an attractive additional short hike leads south toward North Peak along a wide ramp parallel to the aforementioned cliff, which diminishes in height as one proceeds. Soon there is no cliff left, and it's an easy stroll over to the edge, from which there's a view down to the McCabe Lakes and beyond toward distant peaks. Immediately in front rises the dark wall of North Peak, now so close that it is overwhelming.

## SHEPHERDS CREST (12,015)

Back in the Nineteen Twenties, François Matthes was working for the U.S. Geological Survey, deciphering the geological history of the Yosemite Region. In his explorations he clambered up Shepherds Crest, and there discovered a curious feature which he described in a well-known article as 'The Little Lost Valley of Shepherds Crest.'[*] This valley was formed in the sediments of an ancient landscape, long before the Sierran uplift. When that uplift occurred, the little valley was nudged upwards, and exists as a remnant on Shepherds Crest, high enough to have avoided glacial sculpturing. Similar little lost valleys can be found on other mountains, notably North Peak, as echoes of an earlier age.

[*]Sierra Club Bulletin, 1933, 68-80, and 1949, 82-86

North Peak From Summit of Shepherds Crest

From Secret Lake, Shepherds Crest rises temptingly close by, just overhead, but actually about another thousand feet higher. From the lake two available routes are: (1) Take the backpackers' route to the McCabe Lakes as far as the top of the aforementioned cliff, and then rock-scramble up the shoulder of the mountain to the summit. (2) Go up a gully to the right of the above route to meet a fairly steep snow slope leading to the base of the shoulder, and then, as above, reach the summit.

We have done the second route, and recommend sturdy mountain boots with lug soles for kicking steps, and an ice axe for added stability. In late morning the sun has softened the snow for easier step-making, but it is helpful to return before afternoon shade hardens it.

Note: Mount Excelsior (12,446). This summit north of Shepherds Crest is also available from the Secret Lake area. Even with the water taxi, it requires a long day from the trailhead at Saddlebag Lake. We once did it with a head start from a campsite in Twenty Lakes Basin. It's never crowded on top. One can enjoy the view like Alexander Selkirk, solitary monarch of all he surveyed.

## TWENTY LAKES BASIN CIRCUIT

This hike involves relatively little gain and loss of elevation, and, by taking advantage of the round trip boat taxi on Saddlebag Lake, can be done in half a day. However, by including the circuit of Saddlebag, it can stretch out to a leisurely full day, a delight for botany buffs, rock-hounds, fishermen -- just one lake after another.

Early in the season and after a heavy winter snowfall, much of the route between Odell and Steelhead will be under snow and obscure. Under these conditions it is mostly cross-country by landmark and map. Thus a mid- or late-season trip may be preferable.

View South From Below Summit, Mount Excelsior

At the fork in the trail just beyond the ranger's cabin at the upper end of Saddlebag Lake, take the right-hand branch marked to Lundy Canyon. Shortly you will pass Hummingbird Lake and reach Lundy Pass (hardly noticeable as a pass), then go by Odell Lake and drop down (rather rocky footing) to Helen Lake. At its outlet the trail branches: to the right, down Lundy Canyon; to the left, continuing the circuit of Twenty Lakes Basin.

Note: Lundy Canyon. At times the sign to Lundy Canyon mentioned above warns as to the condition of this trail. The canyon portion is steep and can be hazardous to the hiker. It may be completely covered with snow. In some seasons, slides have obliterated sections of the trail. Check with the forest service or at Saddlebag Lake Resort to learn the current conditions before starting down.

To continue the circuit of Twenty Lakes Basin, take the left branch around the north side of Helen Lake. The trail is not on the topo, but is mostly well-defined. (The Twenty Lakes Basin map shows a trail going around the *south* side of Helen Lake; it would be quite awkward.) Passing a flowery meadow to the right of a small waterfall, the trail ascends to Shamrock Lake. Some of this is often snow-covered, even late in the season. Along the way are fine views of the snowy peaks to the west. Pass Excelsior Lake and cross the outlet of Steelhead Lake to reach the old mining road which takes you back to Saddlebag to complete the circuit.

To enjoy the best mountain views, go in the direction of Lundy Pass as described, so that on the stretch between Helen and Steelhead the snowy mountains are in view.

## MEANDERING THE BASIN

Sometimes you may feel an urge not to follow a trail at all, to have no specific destination, but to amble uphill and down in blissful indecision. Here are two suggestions:

Meander One: From the upper end of Saddlebag Lake there's a fascinating broken-up landscape between the trail to Lundy Canyon and the old mining road trail to Steelhead Lake. The rocky terrain is pocked with lakes bearing picturesque names like Hidden Golden, Little Steelhead, and Z. Many others are not even named on the Twenty Lakes Basin map. Fishermen wander from one of these 'hidden' lakes to another, but the scene is equally enjoyable to photographers and all varieties of mountain enthusiasts for a few hours, half a day, or all day long -- take your choice.

Meander Two: Another fine area, and remarkably different from the one just described, is west of the old mining road between Greenstone Lake on the south and Steelhead and Cascade Lakes on the north. It is mostly formed of bright shining granite, decorated with clumps of whitebark pine, and glaciated into broad sweeping pavements -- in striking contrast to the dark, crater-like contours of Meander One. This can be the beginning of a life-long love affair with Cathedral Peak granodiorite. A high level meander is between Cascade Lake southwards to the Conness Lakes, and so on back to Saddlebag Lake.

Less than a meander, more than a stroll, is a visit to the mine just above Steelhead Lake. It is at the terminus of the old mining road where the rusty tailings are clearly visible on the hillside above the lake. This tungsten mine belonged to Gus Hess, one of the first settlers in Lee Vining. He married a local woman and founded the first school in Lee Vining for the education of his and his neighbors' children. The mine operated for many years before it closed. During the Second World War it was re-opened but was closed shortly thereafter.

Arctic Willow (*Salix arctica*)

# 7. ADDITIONAL HIKES AND WALKS ALONG THE TIOGA ROAD

Mount Dana Quad, 40', 7.5"
Tioga Pass Quad, 40', 7.5"

## 'SUNSET KNOB' (10,018')

Just across the road from the Tioga Lake Campground, a hillside slants up several hundred feet eastward, terminating in a light-colored dome-shaped rock. If one happens to be staying at the campground, and a spectacular sunset is in the offing, this is a fine spot from which to enjoy it. Noted on the topo as 10,018', but unnamed, we have dubbed it 'Sunset Knob'.

In addition to the lakeside parking just outside the campground, there is another limited space across the road and a short distance uphill. This is the starting point for going up the slope toward the knob. On the rocks, bright blue whorled pentstemon contrasts beautifully with yellow mountain sulfur flower.

Underfoot the light-colored aplite bedrock is polished by glaciers and broken up by time. Along the way to the left is a grove of husky lodgepole pines, and in their midst, a tall multi-trunked whitebark, very old and weather-beaten. To better appreciate its size and twisted form, go around its west side. At the base in midsummer blooms a garden of golden arnica. A bit farther up are clusters of sunflower-like mule ears.

Kuna Crest From 'Sunset Knob'

It takes only ten or fifteen minutes to reach 'Lower Sunset Knob', surmounted by a rock cairn. Already a broad view opens up, especially of Dana and more distant Kuna Crest across Tioga Lake.

'Upper Sunset Knob' (about twenty minutes further) provides a much more panoramic view. Drop down a bit to the saddle separating the two knobs and bear left to the shoulder for a better gradient and footing than heading straight for the top. Along the way are some old prospectors' diggings.

The mountain air is perfumed by a fragrant mix of mountain sagebrush, pungent wax currant, pennyroyal, and the rosy-cream blossoms of the well-named prickly phlox.

At the top and just over the northern edge grows a clump of graceful mountain hemlocks, often found where seeps provide a little more water. Immediately below, Bennettville's two cabins appear among the trees. Linger for sunset over Mount Conness to the northwest and the sweeping view across Tioga Lake to Dana and Kuna Crest, all bathed in alpenglow -- a fitting end to a perfect mountain day.

## TIOGA LAKE CIRCUIT

From the campground, simply follow the fishermen's trail around the lake – a little farther than it looks, but a pleasant walk almost entirely on the level. In some sections the trail is poorly defined.

## NUNATAK NATURE TRAIL

For the motorist who is looking for a break from an arduous day's driving, this is an ideal breather. Just to get out in the cool spicy air and stretch the legs and lungs for half an hour or more can be a welcome relief.

The Nunatak Nature Trail starts in a spacious parking area located 1.7 miles east of Tioga Pass on the left (north) side of the road. It is almost level and can be covered in about fifteen minutes, but deserves at least twice that time. A few feet along the way are some picnic tables, and further along, benches for contemplation.

The trail circles around several small tarns in a mixed forest of lodgepole and whitebark pines  Dana and Tioga Peak dominate views across the tarns, and for immediate backdrop there is a cliff of orange-brown bedrock shot through with white aplite dikes. High on a tree by the larger tarn is a sign, 'Lake Glenn.'

Along the water's edge grow silver willow and those circumpolar migrants from the northland, fireweed and red heather. In the meadows are moisture-loving shooting stars and elephant heads, yet on the rocks immediately adjacent, dry-habitat plants like mountain sulfur flower, whorled pentstemon, and nude buckwheat.

Mountain chickadees are often busy in the trees, as well as chipmunks and ground squirrels dashing back and forth between lake, meadow, and forest -- all of them gathering winter supplies and incidentally planting and fertilizing this natural garden.

A *nunatak* is an area (like the top of Mount Dana and Dana Plateau) which remained free of ice in the midst of surrounding glaciers.  Many beautiful and informative etched metal signs – works of art – help the visitor to imagine the natural history of this glaciated area: how the plants  found refuge during glacial times on the *nunataks* above, and returned to re-colonize the area after the glaciers retreated.  And how the birds and animals help the plants to grow and reproduce. This seemingly static mountain world has been constantly changing through the millenia. A sign quotes one of John Muir's most famous passages:

> *It is hard to realize the magnitude of work done on these mountains during the last glacial period by glaciers, which are only streams of closely compacted snow crystals…In the development* [of the mountains] *Nature chose for a tool…the tender snowflakes noiselessly falling through unnumbered centuries, the offspring of the sun and sea.*

Reading this, and looking about, one can easily believe that the glaciers melted back only yesterday, and so they did. Since then trees have been reestablished, the whitebarks planted by that noisy local inhabitant, the Clark's nutcracker. The cones don't readily open and the seeds don't have wings, but the nutcracker extracts and hides some 32,000 pine nuts a season, in caches of four or five. He only retrieves seventy per cent, leaving the rest to sprout. The trees depend on the birds, and the birds on the trees.

## ELLERY LAKE DAM TRAIL

This short walk is unique in providing an opportunity to see flowers that typically grow at timberline or above, at a much lower elevation. Indeed, this is the lowest elevation we have ever seen alpine gold or alpine columbine in bloom.

The area is popular with fishermen who line up along the dam, frequently braving a strong wind to land a string of trout.

To get started, park at the lower end of Ellery Lake, 3.2 miles east of Tioga Pass. Walk across the dam at the outlet. Once across, turn left onto a rough construction/maintenance road, between two walls of willows.

The end of the trail is about fifteen minutes away at a slightly higher point, but it is worth spending at least an hour on the round trip. The road was carved out along a talus slope of enormous granite boulders and there is fine glacial sculpturing on the cliffs above and the polished bedrock below. There are spectacular views both up into 'Ellery Cirque' and down the Lee Vining Canyon to the Tioga Road, a highway that was an engineering feat, where cars seem to crawl like ants.

This walk is notable because of the variety of alpine plants, both those that depend upon moisture like labrador tea and red and white heather, and those that usually inhabit the peaks, such as the alpine gold and columbines mentioned above. Phlox, pyrrocoma, and several kinds of daisies pave the route. An easy walk with many satisfactions, especially for those who love the high country flora.

Note: 'Ellery Cirque' is the broad amphitheater soaring skyward two thousand feet above Ellery Lake to the rim of Dana Plateau. Lower down are many huge talus boulders; higher up, steep ice and snow. An invitation for well-equipped and able climbers – a direct route to Dana Plateau.

A curious feature of the cirque is how the left half is pale granite, and the right half, dark metamorphic rock which sweeps downward in a purplish fan across the base.

For years when Carl Sharsmith was conducting alpine botany seminars, he used to take his students a distance up the talus slope to some large boulders. There in the shadow of the rocks where the sun never shines grows a rare saxifrage, a hangover from the ice age.

## WARREN CANYON

After days in the brilliant glare of fellfields and peaks, a short hike up Warren Canyon provides a welcome spell of forest shade and soft lighting.

4.6 miles east of Tioga Pass is a parking area on the right side of the road. Opposite is a gated rough road that turns into a trail going up Warren Canyon. At first, for a short distance, the trail is awash with a side stream on its way to Warren Creek. The trail ascends very gradually, alternately through wet meadows and shady groves. The wet meadows have an especially lush growth of flowers like rein orchis, wild geranium, red lily, and larkspur.

Shooting Star, *Dodecatheon alpinum*

## MOUNT WARREN (12,327')

A striking fact about the first ascents of various Sierra peaks in our area is the large discrepancy in their dates. For example, Dana and Gibbs were both climbed in the 1860's (as long ago as the Civil War), whereas North Peak was not climbed until 1937 (as recently as the Great Depression). Mount Warren falls into the first category as it was first climbed in 1868 just after the Civil War, by a Mr. Wackenreyder.

Today, the easiest routes are from roadheads well up on the east side of the mountain. As is frequently the case, these steep rough roads were built to service mining ventures. And, of all things, a Los Angeles Boy Scout wilderness camp is located up there. So, in thumbing through the summit register, one notes many a Boy Scout sign-up.

A bit more of a wilderness adventure is a route from the west side. We have done this several times. It involves an elevation gain of over three thousand feet, somewhat more than doing Dana from Tioga Pass.

Park, as mentioned above, for hiking into Warren Canyon. After about three-quarters of a mile along the trail, it is time to start up the east side of the canyon. A study of the Mount Dana Topo indicates a rather flat meadow area on a bench about seven or eight hundred feet above the canyon floor. This is the first objective. It can be reached by ascending somewhat to the right of a stream which flows from the above meadow down to Warren Creek. This part of the climb involves the most bushwacking.

Upon reaching the meadow (which is very attractive and has fine views towards Tioga Peak), follow the stream to where it emerges from a wide gully that slants fairly sharply for over a thousand feet up the mountain. Ascend it. Higher up it narrows, and leads out to another much flatter area. Just ahead to the left is a summit. This is not Mount Warren. Continue beyond it to the

View Southwest From Summit, Mount Warren

right until you can see the true mountain top. Once more the gradient steepens; proceed to the rocky summit, and take in the sweeping view down to Mono Lake, a jeweled mirror in a desert setting.

In marked contrast with the atmosphere of a forlorn mining camp to be found on the east side, the area just before the summit on the south side (the route traversed) has a marvelous wild remote quality.

For our initial climb of Warren, we, along with some bumbling, worked out the above route and considered it a fine day. Then we became more ambitious. What about an overnight backpack, sleeping out on top, witnessing the sunset, the summer stars, sunrise over Mono Lake the next morning?

Why not pick a date for full moon? That would be a fine adventure. (We had previously done this sort of thing on Mount Whitney, exciting but mighty chilly.)

And so, having a clearer image of just how to find our way, and prepared for below-freezing temperatures, we loaded our Keltys and were off. Truly, with packs it was more laborious, but we made it. Mono Lake was graced with dreamy cloud reflections and the sunset was a fiery gold. However, our plan of sleeping on top became dubious – the summit was a mass of layered rocks turned on jagged ends. Just the ticket for a masochist!

We retreated ignominiously, dropping down a couple of hundred feet on the east side to a luxurious sandy flat, sheltered by gnarled whitebark pines. Soon an unbelievably huge golden moon rose over the lake. Later it turned so silvery bright that we could hardly sleep.

We were wakened by bright morning sun on our faces, and cooked a quick breakfast of oatmeal and prunes, before rolling up our sleeping bags and starting downhill.

Rather than returning as we had come, the Boy Scout route down the southeast side of the mountain looked easier and would be a completely new hike for us. We started down cross-country, and in due time reached the Tioga Road close by the ranger station, a descent of about five thousand feet, equal to the drop from the South Rim of the Grand Canyon to the Colorado River. Our knees were feeling it.

Looking forward to grabbing a quick hitch back to our car at the Warren Creek parking, we started walking along the road, waving our thumbs at every passing vehicle. To our surprise and chagrin, no one picked us up. These two middle-aged backpackers armed with dangerous-looking ice axes must have intimidated the passing motorists, who stepped on the gas and sped away.

We trudged on until, after seemingly endless hours, we had covered the entire 6.3 miles back to our car, gaining about two thousand feet. Adding this to the five thousand feet mentioned above, we had achieved seven thousand feet difference in elevation in a single day. Back at our Tioga Lake Campground, several wine punches did ease the weariness. As Richard Haliburton put it, a glorious adventure!

Note: Lee Vining Peak (11,690): At first, this is a rough cross-country bushwack with poor footing. Later on it is easy going At the start of the trail up Warren Canyon, turn right and scramble up through sagebrush, buck-brush, and mountain mahogany to the foot of a conspicuous gully. Climb the gully,. Once through the notch onto the shoulder, there is easy footing across spacious meadows with diminishing trees to the summit of Lee Vining Peak. Quite the opposite of Mt. Whitney — there's a good chance you will meet nobody on top. The view into Mono Basin and across Mono Lake is all yours.

# 8. THE MONO PASS REGION

Koip Peak Quad: 40', 7.5"
Sketch Map # 6

In the distant past, long before the first white men came to the Sierra, Paiute peoples from the Great Basin used this pass as a route to the land of the Miwoks on the western slope. They carried salt and dried brine-fly pupae (*kutsavi*) from Mono Lake and obsidian from its craters to trade for acorns to eke out their winter food supplies. In their yearly treks across the mountains, they came to regard the Mono Pass area as sacred, and so it is to this day.

In recent years they have begun to walk the trail again, not for trade but in recognition of their history and as an expression of their identity as a people. Once each summer the Mono Paiutes and their friends, both Native American and white, trek up Bloody Canyon, over the pass, and all the way to Yosemite Valley – men and women, boys and girls, young and old.

One season we met them as they came singing and carrying banners on their joyous pilgrimage. Their enthusiasm and love of the mountains imparted to us latter-day pilgrims a new sense of the holiness of the land.

Far less holy, and leaving heavier footsteps, were the crusty prospectors who, less than a hundred fifty years ago, came with pick axe rather than ice axe, seeking the ever-elusive Mother Lode which would transform their life of deprivation and hardship to one of fantastic wealth and luxury.

So, when you take the ancient Mono Trail, there is excitement in knowing that generations beyond imagining have trod this path before you.

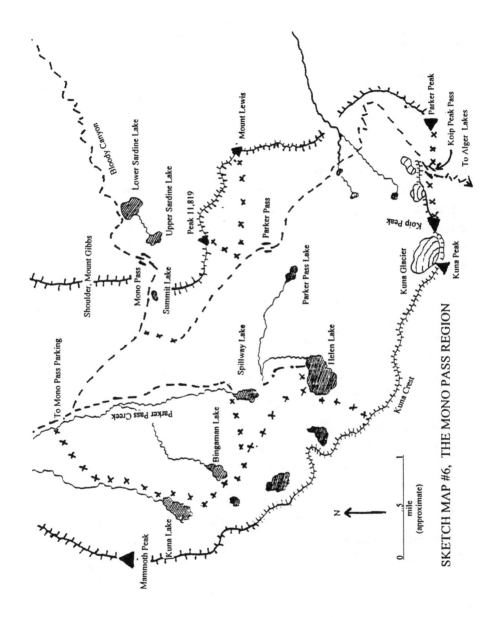

SKETCH MAP #6, THE MONO PASS REGION

## MONO PASS AND BLOODY CANYON

To include the descent of Bloody Canyon, it is necessary (assuming a one-day trip) to have a car shuttle at a roadhead in the Walker Lake area at the base of Bloody Canyon.

Depart from the Mono Pass trailhead located about 1.5 miles west of the Tioga Pass Entrance Station on the south side of the road, with multiple parking places and a restroom.

Shortly, after passing a lakelet (or meadow, depending upon the season) with a splendid close-up view of Mammoth Peak, cross Dana Fork. The trail leads alternately through lodgepole pine forest and across lush meadows that open up the view of the surrounding mountains. Something over an hour from the start is a junction, the left branch signed to Mono Pass, the right branch to Spillway Lake. Take the left-hand branch uphill through the forest. Along the way there's a conspicuous talus slope where pikas are frequently heard and seen. Emerging from the forest, you face a spacious meadow upland rimmed by shining mountains, especially Kuna Crest to the west. A short distance further are Mono Pass and Summit Lake.

Here at Summit Lake, the youthful John Muir camped for a night in the summer of 1869. As the wind rose, his fire 'squirmed and struggled as if ill at ease.' Suddenly the full moon rose over the cliff wall. 'She seemed to be just on the rim of Bloody Canyon looking only at me. This was indeed getting near to Nature...I might say I never before had seen the moon.'

Nearby are the abandoned diggings of the Golden Crown Mine with remains of several cabins still standing. Here, through the winter of 1882-3, the Mount Gibbs Mining Company kept some fourteen miners at work, although it is not clear whether any silver was actually extracted. Remnants of cloth show that the miners actually lined the walls with whatever fabrics they could nail up to help keep out the cold. Artists find irresistible these weathered log relics standing in starkly magnificent surroundings.

Corn Lily, *Veratrum californicum*

A Golden Crown Mine Cabin Near Mono Pass

(Note: From Mono Pass, the topo reveals another readily accessible route up Mount Gibbs, just an extended rocky scramble up the southern shoulder. A gain of just over two thousand feet puts one on top. Here and there along the way are abandoned mining claims and diggings, evoking a sense of the endless exertions of long-ago prospectors. The most convenient descent is by the route described on page 44, which meets the Mono Pass Trail near the Dana Fork crossing.)

Just down from Mono Pass is Upper Sardine Lake, and much further down, Lower Sardine Lake.* On either side, the rugged deep-rose and tawny canyon walls make a spectacular frame for the blue-gray desert beyond. The trail descends rapidly

---

*Named, apparently, for a box of sardines intended for one of the mining camps, that disappeared in the lake when a mule fell off the trail. (Peter Browning, *Place Names of the Sierra Nevada.*)

from the alpine botanical zone at Mono Pass to the great basin flora at Walker Lake, a drop of about twenty-seven hundred feet.

This ancient trail was used by prospectors and others who, unlike the Paiutes before them, used horses and mules. So sharp was the rock and so steep the way that a certain number of animals fell to their death, and many of the survivors were badly cut up. So much blood was spilled on the rocks, they called it Bloody Canyon.

Some years ago we took this route with Carl Sharsmith and several friends. One of our number had left her car at a roadhead below, and as we walked down and down, we were comforted to know we didn't have to come back up the same way.

After a leisurely day and many exciting plant identifications (walking with Carl was always exciting), we came out of the canyon onto a sagebrush flat that sloped grandly downward to the highway far below. We reached Walker Lake -- but no car! After a fruitless search, we went to the resort on the lake and explained our dilemma. The owner laughed. "I know exactly what you did," he said, "and your car's about eight miles away."

He loaded all eight of us into his station wagon and drove us to a *different* roadhead to our missing vehicle. Quite later than planned, we finally arrived in Lee Vining for a bounteous chicken dinner at Nicely's, and still later returned to Tuolumne Meadows. Early the next morning, Carl and three of our party turned up sleepy to start a five-day alpine botany seminar, and that was another adventure. All's well that ends well!

## SPILLWAY LAKE (10,450')

Take the Mono Pass Trail from the previously mentioned parking area, and reach the junction after something over an hour. Then take the well-defined trail to the right signed to Spillway Lake. The route, as earlier, alternates between meadow and forest and the final stretch is along the rushing cascades of Parker Pass Creek, the outlet of Spillway Lake. Here the trail peters out.

Spillway Lake

## HELEN LAKE (10,952')

There are many Helen Lakes in the Sierra. This one is named for Helen Smith, a daughter of George Smith who was a director of the United States Geological Survey. Would you believe that another one was named for Helen of Troy? Yet another, for John Muir's younger daughter. Best to stop here.

To reach the Helen Lake in question from Spillway, it is helpful to orient by the topo and sketch map. Ascend to the right of Helen's outlet stream on a fairly well-defined trail. (From Spillway Lake to the start of the uphill trail to Helen, there is no connecting trail, just cross-country.)

Helen is about five hundred feet higher than Spillway, beautifully situated at the foot of Kuna Crest. Around it grow beds of bright blue timberline pentstemons and dwarf whitebark *krummholz*. Although it is no longer stocked, this clear body of water is popular with fishermen.

Kuna Crest, now close by and mirrored in the water, beckons. It can be reached from Helen Lake by energetic hiking and scrambling. After a thousand foot gain you're on the crest, with grand views in all directions.

One summer some years ago, I (Carroll) and grandson Talmadge, aged 8, were so beckoned -- especially Talmadge. I was hesitant, noting huge cumulo-nimbus clouds piling up. But I wished to encourage the boy's mountain enthusiasm, so up we went to the crest.

The storm clouds above, the dramatic lighting on the mountains below, would have delighted Ansel Adams. We didn't linger, but hurriedly started back. Before we were halfway down to Helen Lake, hail stones the size of mothballs pelted us. Thunder thundered almost instantaneously after the lightning flashed – a bit disconcerting. Something to be said for polytheism at that point. Some of the gods favored us, and hours later – wet, cold, and hungry – we arrived gratefully back at the roadhead. Muir would have called it a great day.

## BINGAMAN LAKE (11,155')

How did it get its name? John W. Bingaman, a Yosemite Park Ranger from 1921 to 1956, tells us: "In 1930 I was a Patrol Ranger in Tuolumne Meadows. I decided to plant an unnamed lake in my district. I took two pack mules loaded with 6,000 rainbow-fry, making a successful plant. By so doing I established the right to call the lake Bingaman." * (If he had been more of a poet, he could have named it Six Thousand Rainbow Lake. Then, as we watch the late afternoon sun sparkle on the water, we could imagine a school of six thousand rainbows simultaneously turning on their sides, reflecting the light.)

To get there, from the lower end of Spillway Lake cross the outlet and climb the hill straight ahead, gaining about seven hundred feet. Turn right and go over rocky open terrain along a high bench below Kuna Crest to Bingaman Lake. It's a pleasure to spend time wandering about the area. For a relatively short cross-country hike from a much-traveled trail, there is a strange feeling of remoteness at this rock-rimmed turquoise gem set down amid a jumble of granite boulders. It breathes an air of solitude and peace.

Note: Instead of returning the same way, if more time is available, try going back by way of Helen Lake. See page 117.

Whitebark Pine
*Pinus albicaulis*

* Bingaman's handwritten statement in YNP files, quoted in Peter Browning's *Place Names of the Sierra Nevada*. It is no longer park policy to plant fish in the lakes.

Easy Slope, Ascending Mount Lewis

## MOUNT LEWIS (12,296')

There's a rough stone cairn on the summit of Mount Lewis, with a metal plaque in memory of W. B. Lewis, Superintendent of Yosemite National Park from 1916 to 1927. The plaque has a strange history. According to Carl Sharsmith, a Boy Scout troop discovered it – on the wrong mountain. They valiantly carried it down and transported it to the proper mountain, where they cemented it firmly in place.

The plaque gives the mountain's elevation as 12,500 feet, quite a bit off from the current topo stating 12,296. In most places the Sierra is said to be still rising, but is Lewis a contrarian mountain? Hardly!

To do Mount Lewis and return, it's best to allow a full day. Although it involves a climb of something less than three thousand feet, the approach is fairly long.

Take the trail to Mono Pass. When you reach the .3 mile sign before the pass, it should also state that this is the junction to Parker Pass which is shown on the map, but it does not do so. Indeed, there is no visible trail leading southerly across the meadow. It has been overgrown. However, the trail can be seen on the opposite hill. Cross the meadow and pick up the trail. It follows a low ridge along which some fantastically shaped whitebark pines frame vistas of the hazy Mono Basin below and beyond.

Well before reaching Parker Pass, the easiest way up Mount Lewis is clearly visible. It is a perfect example of a Class 1 jaunt, just a walk-up, but longer than it looks. Deer browse the grasses and flowers far above timberline and anise swallowtails and white parnassian butterflies flit above. As on most of the peaks, there's an alpine garden of cushion plants like pygmy daisy, several kinds of wild buckwheat, and phlox.

An alternative route to Mount Lewis is from the lower end of Spillway Lake. Go cross-country from there to meet the Parker Pass trail and climb the mountain as described above.

An option or addition to Lewis is Mount 11,805 just to the north of Lewis and above Mono Pass. It is lower and not so far from the trailhead, an easy walk-up, and has a good view down historic and scenic Bloody Canyon.

Parker Pass is one of the flattest passes in the Sierra. Yet it is the divide between the western and eastern watersheds, and also the boundary between Yosemite National Park and Inyo National Forest.

Koip Peak Pass and Koip Peak are beyond Parker Pass. These destinations are for those willing to put in a very long and strenuous one-day hike. They are much more accessible for overnighters.

On one occasion we made this easier choice, camping at one of the snug little lakelets before the zigzags to Koip Peak Pass. Next day, a leisurely climb to the pass and then on to both Koip and Parker Peaks.

It's of historic interest to know that many years ago, Carl Sharsmith used to lead a much more austere one-day hike from Mono Pass Trailhead up Koip Peak Pass to the Kuna Glacier and back – a grueling seventeen mile trip. A special attraction was visiting the ice cave in the glacier.[*] He had no difficulty recruiting enthusiasts.

## HELEN LAKE VIA KUNA AND BINGAMAN LAKES

The jewel of this trip is the extended cross-country traverse along the base of Kuna Crest from Mammoth Peak to the crest above Helen Lake. This is a rocky upland with marvelous views in every direction – just the thing for those who yearn, at least occasionally, to get off busy trails and enjoy some soothing solitude.

---

[*] Since then, the glacier has melted back and the cave has disappeared.

View Southwest From Mount 11,805

However, it is helpful to have some familiarity with the lay of the land in this area, as well as experience with route finding aided by a topo, before undertaking the cross-country section of this trip. Allow a full day.

Take the Mono Pass Trail from the parking area. After about forty-five minutes, on the left, there's an old skeletal cabin of just a few logs. About fifteen minutes later, at the upper end of a small meadow, turn right and cross Parker Pass Creek. Head up through the woods, keeping to the right of the reddish ridge which rises in front of and separate from the wall of Kuna Crest. In time, the outlet stream from Kuna Lake is reached. Follow its course, more or less, to Kuna Lake.

The lake of deep greenish turquoise is cradled in a rocky bowl at the base of a striking unnamed peak that rises almost 1500 feet above it in a sheer granite wall. Usually no one else is around to share it with you. There are some 'fossil' campsites at Kuna Lake which evoke the times before this watershed was closed to camping.*

Heading south, go around the east (left) side of the lake and climb to the next bench, making your way through the least rocky impediments to reach Bingaman Lake. The route from Bingaman to Helen may look daunting, but is not at all difficult. Keeping southward, there's a considerable drop down, then a climb, taking the easiest gradient to the ridge above Helen Lake. (Off to the left is the impressive cliff above Spillway Lake, and off to the right is a higher steeper ridge. But between these is a sort of corridor which leads to the ridge line at a hikeable incline.)

---

*in order to protect the Tuolumne Meadows water supply.

Mount Lyell From Near Kuna Peak

The sole impediment in descending to Helen Lake is the density of the dwarf whitebark, almost like a maze. From Helen's outlet stream, take the trail down to Spillway, where this trail ends. Then go around Spillway to its outlet and join the trail leading back to Tioga Road.

Note: Upon reaching Bingaman Lake, a shorter version of this trip would be to descend to the lower end of Spillway (see page 114) and meet the return trail there.

Obviously this hike can be done in reverse, first going up to Helen Lake. However, the descent from Kuna Lake to Parker Pass Creek to meet the Mono Pass trail can be tricky, not having a point ahead to orient by, as one had coming up to Kuna Lake. Also, towards the end of a long hiking day it is easier to be on a well-defined trail than to be bushwacking cross-country.

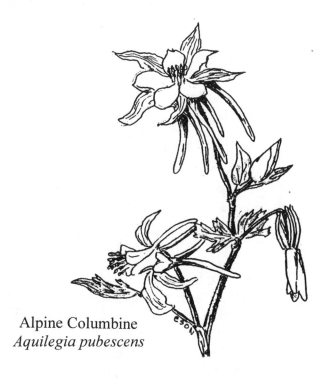

Alpine Columbine
*Aquilegia pubescens*

## 9. MAMMOTH PEAK (12,117)

Vogelsang Peak Quad, 40', 7.5"

Our California Sierra has, not many miles apart, two mammoth mountains. One, the official Mammoth Mountain, is the hub of a world-class ski resort at Mammoth Lakes, California. It is a sleeping volcano which, from time to time, gives hints of waking up. Its shaggy, slaggy hulk is much modified by a variety of ski lifts and has even been re-shaped to present ever-more-enticing ski runs. A gap in the Sierra wall to the west lets through abundant winter storm clouds with their generous deluge of snow flakes – thus, splendid skiing, often as late as the fourth of July. An extra bonus for skiers is the wintry spectacle of Ritter, Banner, and the Minarets etched against the western sky.

The other mammoth mountain, in Yosemite Park close to Tioga Pass, is Mammoth Peak. It is quite a contrast to its close namesake to the south, which is overrun by people. Here, many days can go by without a single person invading the solitude of its summit. Not a dark-complexioned volcano, but mostly a mass of gleaming pale granite, pristine, without any mechanical 'improvements,' It is the northern anchor of Kuna Crest, and to the tourist entering from the east at Tioga Pass, it presents a spectacular view.

Indeed, it is almost irresistible to hikers who love to climb up little-visited peaks. Getting to the top is all cross-country; not a single trail eases the way. A glance at the Vogelsang Peak topo suggests various possibilities: The climb from Lyell Canyon on its

Mammoth Peak Across a Tioga Tarn

western flank is rather steep and requires about a 3300 foot elevation gain. From the Mono Pass Trail to the east, one can save about eight hundred fifty feet of elevation gain, but such big rocks to surmount, as an exploration will reveal.

The route we prefer is from an off-road parking area 3.1 miles west of Tioga Pass on the southern side of the road. This involves about six hundred feet less elevation gain than from Lyell Canyon, and has easier rock to deal with than from the Mono Pass trail.

The sketch above shows the route. The idea is to head for the indicated notch along the northwest shoulder of the mountain. First, the job of wading across Dana Fork which, early in the season, is both cold and swift. Later in the summer it's much easier. Go up through the deep shady woods to timberline. Avoid getting entangled in thick stands of willow. Once you're in the open, the skyline notch is clearly visible. Head toward it, up impressive down-sloping glacier-polished granite slabs. However, before reaching the notch, turn left and traverse eastward below the ridge line but above much steeper rocks – easier than through the whitebark thickets along the ridge line.

In time, moving upward as well as eastward over a jumbled rocky slope, you reach an upper, much flatter sandy area just below the summit. This is a place of shining rock crystals and beautiful alpine plants: alpine gold, butter balls, ivesia, etc.

The easiest route to the top is at the south end. Thread your way upward around the rocks and fragrant lupines. Finally, a splendid view, especially of the Lyell Group to the south.

The odds are that no one else will be en route or on the summit. No Mammoth Mountain, this! Yet we have had several improbable encounters up there. Once naturalist Michael Ross and his wife, Lisa, suddenly appeared as we were having lunch on top.[*] Another lunchtime, we looked down the steep, bouldery east slope to see Laurie Lawrence, another High Sierra afficionado, bounding up the rocks. On two other occasions we met Bud from the Tuolumne Meadows Mountain Shop. All of us on these occasions were equally surprised and pleased to share a lovely mountain day.

Yet another experience was even more improbable. Many summers over a number of years, we had signed the register and made a few brief remarks. The next time we opened it, we found that a couple of guys from the Bay Area had left us a note: "Betty and Carroll, X X X. You sound like our kind of girls. Give us a buzz at # ---, and maybe we can get together." We could not help smiling at this gender confusion, and somewhat reluctantly we did not respond, for that would have destroyed a pleasant daydream. Nicer to let it live on as one of those elusive might-have-beens.

[*] For many years, on his day hikes, Mike has introduced the natural world to numerous Tuolumne Meadows visitors.

Lyell Group From Near Summit, Mammoth Peak

When returning, upon reaching the area of the notch, take a sighting on 'Gaylor Ridge' as a guide in the descent, in order to come out at the parking area on the highway. Avoid a natural tendency, due to the lay of the land, to drop down too far to the left and miss the parking area altogether.

Timberline Sagebrush

(*Artemisia rothrockii*)

# AFTER-THOUGHT

Writing this book has evoked for us memories of innumerable happy days spent in the mountains we love best. The photographs were taken at different times and with different companions: daughters, grandchildren, good friends. Yet the mountains remain. They are constantly changing, but on a time scale so much greater than the span of our lifetime that they seem eternal. For us, Mount Dana will always rise above its lake-spangled meadows, and on its slopes the polemonium will always bloom. As you walk these trails and see the many beauties along them, may it be the same for you!

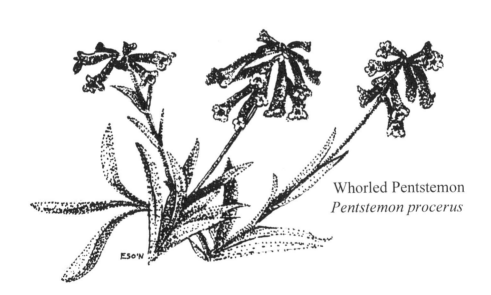

Whorled Pentstemon
*Pentstemon procerus*

# REFERENCES

Note: The Visitors' Centers mentioned on page 13 are excellent sources of books and pamphlets concerning the Sierra Nevada, both its natural history and its human history. This is also true of the Visitors' Center in Yosemite Valley.

Arno, Stephen. *Discovering Sierra Trees*. Yosemite and Sequoia Natural History Associations, 1986. (Eminently portable, fine illustrations by Jane Gyer.)

Botti, Stephen J. *An Illustrated Flora of Yosemite.* Beautifully illustrated by Walter Sydoriak. Yosemite Association, 2001. (Weighing in at much too much for a field guide, but a handsome and definitive volume for leisurely reference and enjoyment.)

Botti, Stephen J. "A Summer Day on the Alpine Desert," YOSEMITE, Vol.48, #4, Fall, 1986. (A delightful botanical excursion on Dana Plateau. Available for examination in the Yosemite Research Library.)

Brewer, William H. *Up and Down California in 1860-1864*. University of California Press, 1949. California Library Reprint Series, 1975.

Browning, Peter. *Place Names of the Sierra Nevada 2$^{nd}$ Edition.* Wilderness Press, 1992.

Clausen, Jens. *The Harvey Monroe Hall Natural Area.* Stanford: The Carnegie Institution of Washington, 1969.

Farquhar, Francis P. *History of the Sierra Nevada.* University of California Press, 1965.

David Gaines. *Birds of Yosemite and the East Slope.* Lee Vining, CA: Artemisia Press, 1992. (See comment, page 138.)

Garth, John S., and Tilden, J.W. *Yosemite Butterflies.* The Lepidoptera Foundation, 1963.

Grater, Russell K. *Discovering Sierra Mammals.* Yosemite and Sequoia Natural History Associations, 1987.

Hickman, James C., Editor. *The Jepson Manual, Higher Plants of California.* University of California Press, 1993. (Too weighty for a field guide, but at present the definitive work on California flora.)

Hill, Mary. *Geology of the Sierra Nevada.* Berkeley: University of California Press, 1975.

Hubbard, Douglass. *Ghost Mines of Yosemite.* Awani Press, Fredericksburg, TX., 1918.

Horn, Elizabeth L. *Sierra Nevada Wildflowers.* Mountain Press, 1998.

Huber, N. King. *The Geologic Story of Yosemite National Park.* U.S. Geological Survey Bulletin #1595, 1987. Yosemite Association, 1989.

Johnston, Verna R. *Sierra Nevada, The Naturalist's Companion.* University of California Press, 1998. (See especially Chapter 6: Tree Line and Beyond. An excellent description of the alpine environment, and its plants and animals.)

LeConte, Joseph. *A Journal of Ramblings Through the High Sierras of California by the University Excursion Party, 1875.* Reprint by Yosemite Association, 1994.

Matthes, François. "The Little Lost Valley on Shepherds Crest". Sierra Club Bulletin 1933, 65-80; also 1949, 82-86.

Muir, John. *My First Summer in the Sierra.* (Copyright 1911 by John Muir.) Houghton Mifflin, 1998.

Munz, Philip A. *California Mountain Wildflowers.* University of California Press, 1963. (A portable field guide not requiring technical skill; a good starter.)

Norris, Robert M., and Webb, Robert W. *Geology of California, $2^{nd}$ Edition.* Wily Publishing Co., 1990. (Another tome for at-home study.)

O'Neill, Elizabeth Stone. *Meadow in the Sky, A History of Yosemite's Tuolumne Meadows Region, $3^{rd}$ Edition.* Albicaulis Press, Groveland, CA 1993.

O'Neill, Elizabeth Stone. *Mountain Sage, The Life Story of Carl Sharsmith, Yosemite's Famous Ranger/Naturalist, $2^{nd}$ Edition.* Albicaulis Press, Groveland, Ca: 1996.

O'Neill, Elizabeth Stone. "Walking With Carl." *SIERRA,* May/June. 1991, 66-69.

Peterson, Roger Tory. *A Field Guide to Western Birds, Revised Edition.* Houghton Mifflin, 1990.

Reedy, Edward, and Granholm Stephen. *Discovering Sierran Birds.* Yosemite Association, 1985.

Roper, Steve. *The Climber's Guide to the High Sierra.* Sierra Club Publisher, 1976.

Sharsmith, Carl. *A Contribution to the History of Alpine Flora of the Sierra Nevada.* Unpublished PhD thesis. University of California at Berkeley, 1940.

Starr, Walter A., Jr. *Starr's Guide to the John Muir Trail and the High Sierra.* A Sierra Club Totebook, $12^{th}$ revised edition, 1974. (Still in print.)

Stebbins, Robert C. *Western Reptiles and Amphibians, $2^{nd}$ Edition.* A Peterson Field Guide, Houghton Mifflin, 1985.

Storer, Tracy I. and Usinger, Robert L. *Sierra Nevada Natural History: An Illustrated Handbook.* University of California Press, 1963. (Still in print.)

Terres, John K. *The Audubon Society Encyclopedia of American Birds.* 1980. (Not a field guide – too heavy – but contains an immense amount of information on American birds.

Weeden Norman. *A Sierra Nevada Flora.* Wilderness Press, 1996. (Works best for a person with some technical skill in using botanical keys.)

Whitney, Stephen. *A Sierra Club Naturalist's Guide: The Sierra Nevada.* Mountaineers, 1987. (See especially Chapter VII, Roof of the Range: Alpine Communities. A fine discussion of the adaptations of plants and animals to an alpine environment.)

# LIST OF ILLUSTRATIONS

| | |
|---|---|
| Gaylor Peak Across Upper Gaylor Lake | Cover |
| The Authors on the Summit of Mount Dana | Back Cover |
| Elizabeth with Carl Sharsmith on the Trail | 3 |
| Carl Sharsmith | 4 |
| Ferdinand Castillo | 4 |
| Pygmy Daisy, *Erigeron pygmaeus* | 5 |
| Anise Swallowtail | 11 |
| Clark's Nutcracker | 16 |
| Mountain Garter Snake | 19 |
| Sketch Map #1, Gaylor and Granite Lakes Basin | 21 |
| On the Summit of Gaylor Peak | 22 |
| Dana City Mine Cabin, circa 1960 | 25 |
| White Mountain from 12,002, Conness Beyond | 28 |
| Alpine Gold, *Hulsea algida* | 29 |
| Sketch Map #2, The Mount Dana Region | 31 |
| Larkspur, *Delphinium glaucum*, and Rufous Hummingbird | 32 |
| Mount Dana From the Lying Head | 34 |
| Gray-crowned Rosy Finch | 36 |
| Northeast Face of Dana From Dana Plateau | 39 |
| Mount Dana Across Icy Tarn on Dana Plateau | 40 |
| Rock Formation, Dana Plateau | 42 |
| Golden-mantled Ground Squirrel | 43 |
| Rock Wren | 45 |
| Dana from Summit of Mount Gibbs | 46 |
| Sketch Map #3, The Mine Creek and Slate Creek Regions | 49 |
| Bennettville | 51 |
| Glacial Erratic near Bennettville | 53 |
| Mount Conness Across Shell Lake | 55 |
| 'Cordwood Ridge' | 57 |
| Dwarf Paintbrush, *Castilleja nana* | 59 |
| Mountain Chickadee | 61 |
| Sketch Map #4, Tioga Crest, Saddlebag Lake | 63 |
| Hermit Thrush | 65 |

| | |
|---|---:|
| 12,002 and White Mountain Across Gardisky Lake | 66 |
| Dana from the Summit of Tioga Peak | 69 |
| Doré Cliff | 71 |
| Arnica, *Arnica sp.* | 72 |
| Research Station, Carnegie Institute, Slate Creek Valley | 75 |
| White Mountain from 'Coyote Ridge' | 77 |
| Kestrel | 78 |
| California Gull | 80 |
| Sketch Map #5, Twenty Lakes Basin | 81 |
| Hyla Treefrog | 82 |
| Timberline Pentstemon, *Pentstemon davidsonii* | 84 |
| Mount Conness From Shoulder of North Peak | 85 |
| Mount Conness From Summit of North Peak | 87 |
| North Peak Across Secret Lake | 89 |
| North Peak from Summit of Shepherds Crest | 91 |
| View South from Below Summit, Mount Excelsior | 93 |
| Arctic Willow, *Salix arctica* | 95 |
| Kuna Crest From 'Sunset Knob' | 97 |
| Shooting Star, *Dodecatheon alpinum* | 101 |
| View Southwest From Summit, Mount Warren | 103 |
| Sketch Map #6, The Mono Pass Region | 107 |
| Corn Lily, *Veratrum californicum* | 109 |
| A Golden Crown Mine Cabin Near Mono Pass | 110 |
| Spillway Lake | 112 |
| Whitebark Pine, *Pinus albicaulis* | 114 |
| Easy Slope, Ascending Mount Lewis | 115 |
| View Southwest from Mount 11,805 | 118 |
| Mount Lyell From Near Kuna Peak | 120 |
| Alpine Columbine, *Aquilegia pubescens* | 121 |
| Mammoth Peak Across Tioga Tarn | 123 |
| Our Route on Mammoth Peak | 124 |
| Lyell Group from Near Summit, Mammoth Peak | 126 |
| Timberline Sagebrush, *Artemisia rochrockii* | 127 |
| Whorled Pentstemon, *Pentstemon procerus* | 128 |
| Shrubby Cinquefoil, *Potentilla fruticosa* | 137 |
| Newberry's Gentian, *Gentiana newberryi* | 140 |
| North Peak Across Greenstone Lake | 142 |

# PLANT LIST

This is only a sampling of the plants which inhabit this rugged high mountain area. (Jens Clausen lists about 350 species in the Hall Natural Area alone.) Curiously, they represent four different origins: species that moved south from higher latitudes (circumpolar), species that moved up-hill from the Pacific slope, ones that moved in from the Rockies and the Great Basin, and some that seem to have evolved right here and survived the ice ages in glacial-free zones (*nunataks*).

Scientific names (in italics) have been checked with *The Jepson Manual of the Higher Plants of California.* Also with *An Illustrated Flora of Yosemite National Park* by Steve Botti.

It is customary to start Latin generic names with capital letters, but not common names. Some High Sierra plants have no common names, or their scientific names are more frequently used, and in these cases, we have included both. It seemed less confusing, for the purpose of this book, not to capitalize any plant names within the text

Many of the genera here listed have multiple species within our area, e.g., the *Castillejas* and the *Pentstemons*. There are several flower field guides to help with identification.

Alpine Gold, *Hulsea algida*
Alpine Goldenrod, *Solidago multiradiata*
Arnica, *Arnica* (several species)
Aspen, *Populus tremuloides*
Bilberry, *Vaccinium caespitosum*
Bistort, *Polygonum bistortoides*
Bog Orchid (Rein Orchid), *Platanthera leucostachys*
Buckwheat, *Eriogonum*
    Butter Balls, *E. lobbii;* Gold Heads, *E. rosense*
    Mountain Sulfur Flower, *E. incanum;*
    Nude Buckwheat, *E. nudum*
    Snow Buckwheat, *E. ovalifolium var. nivale*

Buttercup, *Ranunculus alismifolius, var. arismellus*
Columbine, Alpine, *Aquilegia pubescens;* Crimson, *A. formosa*
Corn Lily, *Veratrum californicum*
Currant, *Ribes cereum*
Daisy (Fleabane), *Erigeron*
      *E. algidus; E. compositus* (both small, on upper slopes)
      *E. coulteri* (Coulter's); *E. peregrinus* (Wandering Daisy)
      *E. pygmaeus* (Pygmy Daisy)
Draba (Mountain Cress), *Draba* (several species)
Elderberry, Mountain Red, *Sambucus racemosa,*
Elephant Heads, *Pedicularis groenlandica, P. attolens*
Fireweed, *Epilobium angustifolium,*
Forget-me-not, *Hackelia micrantha (formerly H. jessicae)*
Gentian, Sierra, *Gentianopsis holopetala*
     Newberry's, *Gentiana newberryi*
Gooseberry, *Ribes montigenum*
Heather, Red, *Phyllodyce breweri*; White, *Cassiope mertensiana*
Hemlock, Mountain, *Tsuga mertensiana*
Ivesia, no common name, *Ivesia* (five species)
Juniper, Dwarf, *Juniperus communis;* Western, *J. occidentalis*
Kalmia (Mountain Laurel), *Kalmia polifolia*
Labrador Tea, *Ledum glandulosum*
Larkspur, *Delphinium glaucum* (and several others)
Lewisia (Bitterroot), *Lewisia* (four species)
Locoweed, *A. whitneyi* (and four other species)
Lupine, *Lupinus*
    Broad-leaved, *L. latifolius*
    Lyall's Lupine, *L. lepidus, var. lobbii (formerly L. lyallii)*
    Dana's Lubin, *L. lepidus, var. danae;*
Meadow Aster, *Aster alpigenus andersonii*
Monkeyflower, *Mimulus*
    Mountain, *M. tilingii;* Primrose, *M. primuloides*
    Suksdorf's, *M. suksdorfii* (a very tiny one)
    Musk, *M. moschatus;* Skunky, *M. mephiticus*
Monkshood, *Aconitum columbianum*
Mountain Oceanspray (Rock Spirea), *Holodiscus microphyllus*

Mule Ears, *Wyethia mollis*
Onion, *Allium*
  *A. obtusum* (small, white); Swamp, *A. validum* (purple)
Paintbrush, *Castilleja*
  Applegate's, *C. applegatei;* Dwarf, *C. nana*
  Great Red, *C. miniata;* Lemmon's, *C. lemmonii*
  Meadow, *C. pearsonii*
Pennyroyal (Indian Tea), *Monardella odoratissima*
Pentstemon (Beard Tongue), *Pentstemon*
  Pride of the Mountain, *P. newberryi;* Showy, *P. speciosus*
  Timberline, *P. davidsonii;*
  Whorled, *P. heteroduxus, P. procerus*
Perideridia (Yampah), *Perideridia bolanderi*
Phlox, *Phlox diffusa, P. condensata*
Pine, Whitebark, *P. albicaulis;* Lodgepole, *P. contorta murrayana*
Podistera (Mountain Parsley), *Podistera nevadensis*
Potentilla (Cinquefoil), *Potentilla*
  Shrubby Cinquefoil, *P. fruticosa* (a bush)
  + seven others, all pale to bright yellow flowers
Prickly Phlox (Granite Gilia), *Leptodactylon pungens*
Pussy Paws, *Calyptridium umbellatum*
Pyrrocoma (Golden Aster, Summer Gold), *Pyrrocoma apargioides*
Raillardella, no common name, *Raillardella scaposa*
Ranger's Buttons, *Sphenosciadium capitellatum*
Rock Fringe, *Epilobium obcordatum*
Rosewort, *Sedum roseum*
Sagebrush, *Artemisia*
  Low, *Artemisia arbuscula;* Timberline, *A. rothrockii*
  + 3 others
Sandwort, *Arenaria aculeata, A. congesta, A. kingii*

Senecio (Groundsel, Ragwort, Butterweed), *Senecio*
    Single-stemmed, *S. integerrimus*
    Arrow-leafed, *S. triangularis*
    Woolly, *S. canus*; *S. scorzonella* (formerly *S. covillei*)
    Meadow, *S. cymbalarioides (*formerly *S. subnudus)*
    Few-flowered, *S. pauciflorus;*
    *S. werneriifolius*, + 2 others
Shooting Star, *Dodecatheon alpinum*
Silvermat, *Raillardella argentea*
Sky Pilot, *Polemonium eximium*
Spiraea, *Spiraea densiflora*
Stonecrop, *Sedum obtusatum,*
Tioga Thistle, *Cirsium scariosum*
Valerian, *Valeriana californica*
Wallflower, *Erysimum capitatum*
Willow, Arctic, *Salix arctica,* Silver, *S. geyeriana*
    Mono, *S. planifolia* (and four others)
Woodland Star, *Lithophragma glabrum*
Yarrow, *Achillea millefolium*

Shrubby Cinquefoil, *Potentilla fruticosa*

# SOME NOTES ON BIRDS IN THE TIOGA PASS REGION

Whatever one's favorite field guide(s) might be, an indispensable addition to maximizing the pleasure of birding in this area is David Gaines' *Birds of Yosemite and the East Slope*. Not a field guide, it is a remarkable survey in depth of the birds of the region: who they are, where and when they are, their abundance or rarity, and much more fascinating material.

Surprisingly for these austere heights, Gaines lists a total of 140 species, only two less than the score for Tuolumne Meadows, which is 1400 feet down-slope. By way of contrast, Mono Lake, just thirteen miles from the pass, comes in with a whopping 279 species – well worth a digression, a day off from the High Country.

Of the 140, some are dedicated mountaineers, while others, just like people, only occasionally visit this rugged terrain. Gaines points out that a number, after the demands of raising a family lower down, take a vacation, as it were, in the high mountains.

Of the ones Gaines lists for the Tioga Pass area, here are forty-one which are more likely to be encountered than the others. The birds who earned a star are the highest nesters – true mountaineers.

    Mallard
    Red-tailed Hawk
    Golden Eagle
    Kestrel
    Prairie Falcon
\*   White-tailed Ptarmigan
    Spotted Sandpiper
    Mountain Quail
    California Gull
    Caspian Tern
    Great Horned Owl
    Rufous Hummingbird

Red-breasted Sapsucker
Hairy Woodpecker
Red-shafted Northern Flicker
Dusky Flycatcher
\* Horned Lark
Steller's Jay
Clark's Nutcracker
Common Raven
Mountain Chickadee
White-breasted Nuthatch
\* Rock Wren
House Wren
American Dipper (Water Ouzel)
\* Mountain Bluebird
Townsend's Solitaire
Hermit Thrush
American Robin
\* Water Pipit
Orange-crowned Warbler
Yellow-rumped (Audubon's) Warbler
Wilson's Warbler
Chipping Sparrow
Mountain White-crowned Sparrow
Oregon Dark-eyed Junco
Brewer's Blackbird
\* Rosy Finch
Pine Grosbeak
Cassin's Finch
Red Crossbill
Pine Siskin
Lesser Goldfinch

# ILLUSTRATION CREDITS

Front cover photograph, Carroll
Back cover photograph, John Tankersley
Cover design, Elizabeth and Carroll
Carl Sharsmith photograph, John O'Neill
Ferdinand Castillo photograph, courtesy of Ferdinand
Sketch maps, Elizabeth and Carroll
All drawings, Elizabeth
Photos on pages: 39, 69, 87, 89, 103, and 115, Elizabeth
All other photos, Carroll

Newberry's Gentian

## ABOUT THE AUTHORS

For over half a century, Carroll and Elizabeth have been hiking and backpacking the High Sierra trails from north of Yosemite to south of Mount Whitney. Some summers were spent farther afield in other ranges: the Alps, Norway, and the Pyrenees; and closer to home, the Cascades and the Canadian and American Rockies. There were shorter trips to Alaska, Mexico, and the Andes. But the mountain range they have loved the best is the California Sierra. This book is a reflection of that love.

For thirty years, they were teachers in Stockton, Elizabeth in various elementary schools, Carroll at Stockton (later Delta) College. During the summers and on occasional sabbatical leaves, they had time for roaming the outdoor natural world.

Carroll graduated from Loyola College in Baltimore, received a Master's degree from the University of Oregon, and did further graduate work at Johns Hopkins and Harvard. Elizabeth graduated from College of the Pacific and received a Master's degree from the University of the Pacific.

They retired to Pine Mountain Lake near Groveland, California, so as to be close to Yosemite National Park and just a couple of hours from Tioga Pass, the hub of the area described in this book. They continue to hike this cherished landscape with children, grandchildren, friends, and of course each other.

Elizabeth has previously published many travel articles in various magazines, and two well-received books: *Meadow in the Sky* and *Mountain Sage*. Carroll's photographs have been used to illustrate a number of her articles and books.

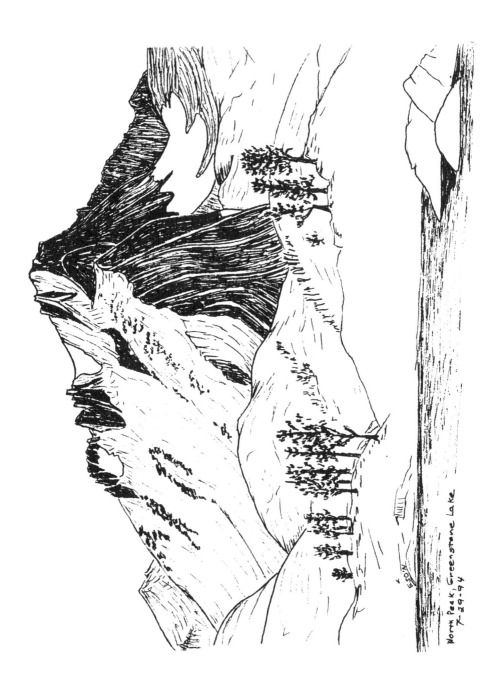